Mike Barnes is an award-winning author whose stories have appeared twice in *Best Canadian Stories*, three times in *The Journey Prize Anthology*, and have won the Silver Medal for Fiction at the National Magazine Awards. He lives in Toronto.

Be With

Letters to a Carer

Mike Barnes

First published in the UK 2019 by
Myriad Editions
www.myriadeditions.com

Myriad Editions
An imprint of New Internationalist Publications
The Old Music Hall, 106–108 Cowley Rd,
Oxford OX4 1JE

First printing
1 3 5 7 9 10 8 6 4 2

Originally published in Canada by Biblioasis

A CIP catalogue record for this book is
available from the British Library

ISBN (pbk): 978-1-912408-18-4
ISBN (ebk): 978-1-912408-19-1

Designed and typeset in Fournier MT

Printed and bound in Denmark
by Nørhaven, Viborg

Be With

Letters to a Carer

Dear ——

Someone told me that your loved one has been diagnosed with Alzheimer's.

I was sorry to hear that, and also a little frightened for you both.

~

I feel I know a few things about you, even before we meet.

Already you are busy beyond belief. Stretched thin, getting by on meagre sleeps. You are sad, frightened, troubled, confused. Dark waves of these emotions estrange you at times from your normal life. But you are also energized, adrenalized. You push down the sadness and the fear to be there for your loved one. To be a voice for, an ally, a companion. To help in every way into this dark.

You are on Caregiver Time. It's like New Parent Time, Student Crunch Time, Double Overtime—all those other stressed and sleepless zones. But Caregiver Time lasts longer. It can last for years. It's lasted seven years, so far, for me.

That's why I'm composing these the way I am. In short bits. Bits I have the time to write, bits you might find the time to read. In a waiting room. During a loved one's nap.

Over takeout coffee in the parking lot.

Messages in bottles.

Uncork on any beach.

~

I also have in mind those packets of dried food people take on long trips into the wilderness. Compact, lightweight nourishment, high in energy and nutrients. Oat bars. Pemmican strips, in olden days.

Pemmican posts?

Read just this. Or, if you like, read several in a row. (It's strange how the over-busy often look for even more to do, from a need for distraction or from the habit of pure speed.) The result may be the same in either case. Your mind crammed and blurry, you'll forget what you read and need to read it again. And that will be a satisfaction, I hope.

Read just this. Put it in your mind like a single pebble in your pocket. Feel it there—small, hard, irregular, with its own peculiar shape—until you have the time to come back for another.

In an hour, a day, a week. A year.

The bits of news, food, stone will still be there.

~

I'm sending you the news I needed to hear myself. Needed and still need often, ransacking confusions to find a clear way forward.

You see, the need for guidance goes back further than my seven years of active caregiving. Since nine years ago, when my mother, Mary, was diagnosed with Alzheimer's—and, really, for some years before that, when something-wrong was obvious but hadn't yet been named—I've had need of the items, soft and hard, that I aim to send here.

Soft: fellowship, solace, understanding.

Hard: facts, clarity, direction.

You need accuracy, but you need kindness too. We all do. Accuracy without kindness is too unfeeling to be true. And kindness without accuracy is too unreal to be felt.

~

"Blah blah blah," Mary says, when stuck in an activity session involving a speaker or storyteller. "Doesn't like to share the stage," says Laura, the activity co-ordinator in her current care home. Partly—and yet, no. Mary transfixes, roots visibly, to a voice speaking; grows intent and still as its currents envelop her. The talk can be about anything, as long as it's just talk. But she has an urchin's antennae for speech designed to edify or placate her.

Forgive me in advance my blah blah blah.

~

Let's try to get a timeline, first. It may be the last thing you want right now. I resisted clock-talk for years myself. Even hearing the word—*timeline*—made me bristle. It belonged to a world of cold quantities that reduced, I felt, individuals with dementia to a kind of grey goo, deteriorating with pre-dictable uniformity as microscopic proteins accumulate in their brains, just as, in that other end-of-the-world scenario, replicating nano-bots turn the particularized universe into mush. Talk of timelines—of *stages* in the *course* of a *disease*—not only equated people with their disease, it gave everyone the same disease. One patient, one disease. That offended me greatly. And was just plain wrong besides. When I meet, as I often do, ten or fifteen people with dementia in a row, they seem as various as any other ten or fifteen people. Maybe they are all moving roughly in the same direction—like caribou moving across a plain from east to west, say, on various meandering paths, some pausing, some even reversing course, but all, after a time, closer to the setting sun than when they began—but the same sense of a shared trajectory can be felt in a nursery, a school classroom, a company cafeteria, a retirement party. People are people, and people are persons, you realize—unless you don't.

I still feel that way. With time, however, I see better the overall direction of dementia, its east-to-westness, and even the somewhat distinct (though still messy and overlapping) stages of its passage. I realize, too, that part of the reason I couldn't see this before was that

I was simply overwhelmed. My twenty-hour caregiving days bombarded me with so many urgent particulars, a great many of them brand new and all of them constantly changing, that I simply lost the ability to see beyond getting through this minute, this hour, this day. Self-protectively, I lost my pattern recognition. Now, with things a little quieter, some of it is coming back.

~

One time (early on, forgotten until just this moment), I was sitting in a corridor with another caregiver, a thin, grey-haired woman, telling her of the micro-naps now riddling my days. Micro-*comas* is more like it. Blacking out for short spells, coming to on the other side. While sitting, while standing. While talking—returning, after sudden dark, a half-sentence or more further on in the conversation. While walking, even —lifting a foot up and putting it down, then noticing I was several steps ahead of where I'd been. Most terribly, while driving.

Gripping the wheel, determined to stay alert—and then popping back, eyes still wide open, further down the highway.

It happened without warning, often when I was unaware of being exceptionally tired. (I was never *not* tired, then.) It was like the gap when a slide projector pushes the current slide out and prepares to push the next slide in. There is a dark interval, which can last for half a second, or be prolonged to a few seconds, or even half a minute or more of oblivion.

This was new to me, and I recounted it with a degree of fascination as well as fright. Perhaps, back then, I was even boasting a little.

The woman sipped her takeout coffee, and said flatly, as of something decided long ago, "You won't be much help to her if you're dead."

~

Mary has moved—I have moved her—four times in seven years. These moves, I see now, map onto the progressive stages of Alzheimer's as clinically described. From mild to moderate, moderate to severe, severe to very severe, very severe to late stage. During the roughly year and a half she lived in each place (sometimes a little more, sometimes a little less), she would be in between stages, leaving one for the next, and the move would become unavoidable when, for example, the moderate-severe stage became more severe than moderate; or when severe-very severe became mostly the latter. The stages are never neat: they are taking place in a person, with all her quirks and qualities; different parts of the brain are affected to different degrees; she is as subject to the vicissitudes of mood and physical health and events of the day and even weather as the rest of us; and she is fighting hard against dementia's encroachments—but in broad outline, especially in retrospect, it is possible to make them out.

And they are the stages, leaving room for digressions, by which I'll organize what I have to tell you.

~

Alzheimer's' beginnings are mysterious. What eventually becomes a great river sweeping all before it may start as thin rivulets wetting grass or leaves deep in a forest half a continent away—origins never to be seen or even guessed at.

Depression mixes with it, mimics it (some deep depressions are called for good reason pseudodementias). Stresses of all kinds play their part. Sleep, diet, alcohol and other drugs, exercise, other daily habits. Physical illnesses and the natural slowing of the ageing brain…

All of these retard or accelerate whatever genetic propensity for dementia is there.

Dementia, like any illness, works with what it has, when it has it. A *person* develops it.

~

The onset of Alzheimer's is sometimes divided into four subtly overlapping phases. Fittingly, the first of these has *no symptoms*. Yet it is still a phase. Those rivulets may be rising in the forest.

Mild Alzheimer's is a rich, and sometimes very long, stage comprising three blended gradations. First, the certain but unmeasurable symptoms of subjective cognitive impairment (SCI). Mary had talked on occasion of feeling "something funny" in her head, and throughout her life, more so in middle years, could be a dreamy, abstracted person, sometimes strangely insistent and repetitious in her stories. Next (and as well), mild cognitive impairment (MCI), measurable on tests but not yet dramatically impacting day-to-day activities. On to (and along with) mild dementia, which does clearly impact daily life and of which all not in denial are aware.

Mary's personality for as long as I've known her (she had me, her first child, at age twenty-nine and she's ninety-one now)—including dreamy and depressive spells, well camouflaged within an active life, a tendency to drift away into alien regions that was part of an intense imagination—shaded gradually into, merged with, the Alzheimer's that was diagnosed when she was eighty-two. There was no definite start, at least not visibly. It was as if those many minute streams accumulated until, obviously, a river was flowing and had been for some time.

At her diagnosis, she felt, she said, "relieved". She had known something was "wrong" with her head for a long time, she said, and it was a relief to finally have it named.

It wasn't her only reaction; typically, she shared only the positive. In an abandoned journal that I found years later in a drawer, she marked that day with just two words.

Dear God

When her husband of sixty years, Bill, my father, died of lung cancer in August 2011, I had been her Power of Attorney for several months, and she was already well along dementia's passage, in the moderate phase that made living alone impossible and made living with others subject to special conditions.

~

I'm saying much more than I planned to. I'm sorry—I can feel your impatience as if by telepathy. Please remember that you can spot-read this in any direction, in any amount. You can, if you dare, practise sortilege, or bibliomancy, by consulting these entries at random.

There's one more thing I want to say at the outset. To set the tone, to state my view of things unequivocally. And to establish something that it's best you hear now, nearer to the start of caregiving—though surely you will need to fight your own way to a belief in it.

It will take a few more entries, I expect, and then I think I can progress with fewer delays.

~

Plainly, so it can't be missed:

All people with dementia, and some of them strikingly, show depths of sensitive awareness, resilience rising to heroism and a capacity for joyful relatedness that is almost totally missing from public discussions of their condition.

~

I could show you a hundred instances of what I mean. Here is one:

It is the morning after I'd finally agreed, after many tense discussions and postponements, to move Mary into a room on the locked ward of the facility she was living in. (This is years up ahead in her story, though still years from its end.) I'd stayed with her until she fell asleep, very late, and returned early with two of the mocha frappuccinos we liked to drink together. Dark circles ring Mary's eyes. When I ask if she slept well, she says, "Oh yes! Very!" Her mood is bright. Mine is glum at best. Space on the locked floor is tight, this room more crammed than her previous one. I wonder what might be added to the storage locker. *The last room. Last but one*, I think. What snares dismay particularly is the two green dumpsters below her window, one floor down. A warm spring day, yet the windows must remain shut. I wonder if adhesive frosting on the lower panes might keep her view just sky.

The faint clanks and thuds from below fascinate her. Startle and fascinate. "What's that?" Her hearing still a wonder.

The garbage truck backing up?

"No. That chim. Not chimney. Chimp."

Chime?

"Yes, chime! Chimp's a monkey!" Her laugh clear and ringing.

She limps over to the window, peers down at the uniformed people pitching bags.

"So many good people. Taking good care ... of us. Of everything."

Large, new homes stretched away around. Yet I knew that, at that moment, not one of them contained a happier person.

~

I know you are imagining what lies ahead. Seeing pictures of a coming desolation and disintegration. I wish I could tell you your pictures are untrue. I can tell you only that they are incomplete. Future's gallery is vaster, more lavish in its paradoxes.

We are so much better at imagining the disasters that lie ahead than we are at imagining the joys. And better at foreseeing both than at perceiving what is already here. We are prepared in some deep way for sorrow. Joy, when it arrives, always breaks in. It interrupts.

I was once in hospital for two years. The first of many serious illnesses, forcing long withdrawals from active life. One day, someone brought me a snack and drink. I opened, with difficulty, the plastic apple juice container. I brought it to my lips, sipped, and—*actually tasted it.* I don't know how else to put it. It felt as natural, and astounding, as waking up. As if I'd simply stepped through a door, across a threshold, and there (here?) I was, aware of all the gifts streaming unearned to me, like milkweed floss on a late summer breeze. *I am warm, I am dry, I have a window to look through (clouds, a couple on a bench).*

Hands, unasked, bring me a mini-muffin and this juice. So sweet, like nectar. Music from a radio down the hall ...

So sanity, as joy, breaks in. Often through the door that insane grief has left ajar.

The taste of apple juice is fleeting. Powerful but delicate, it recedes under a barrage of other tastes and duties. I return to it as often as I can—or *am returned*, since it is not an act of conscious will, but a relaxation of will and a deepening of attention, that takes me back to that place of simple belonging and gratitude.

With Mary, for all that caring for her has cost me, I return to tasting apple juice more often than I do with those who are well, i.e., not suffering from any named impairment. Seeing that she has got there first, ahead of me. Seeing that there is a space cleared in which we may sit together quietly, sipping what is given.

~

Driving to visit Mary the other day, I heard on the car radio an author I admire answering the question, Who is your current hero? My father, she said, who despite advanced dementia still manages to be himself much of the time. (Her words were close to these.)

I felt a surge of agreement, and a trailing need to qualify.

Hero. Yes, absolutely. What do heroes do? They enter dark places upright; fight monsters there; get maimed, sometimes killed; emerge with treasure.

Mary's been my hero for a long time, for my whole life perhaps, but never more so than during these years when I've been her caregiver. She's fought this toughest battle with such abundant heart. I would say she's been my teacher, except that I could never emulate the sheer grit, tenacity, grace and humour she's brought to her ordeal. Almost miraculously, she's kept the essence of herself against a withering assault—yes, I agree with the author on that—but, even more miraculously, she's gone beyond maintaining her old self in order to learn to be a new person, with new and extended abilities—this in her tenth decade, in the teeth of such steep odds.

~

A new person. New abilities.

That flies in the face of what we're told about Alzheimer's and other dementias. Loss, loss, loss and loss is how they're usually described—not without reason.

Dementia is spoken of as a terrible tag-end to the real life that came before it. It strips a person, piece by piece, returning nothing of value.

But that is true only in part, and in no part true enough.

Dementia is certainly terrible; and, being invariably fatal, an end as well. But it is no tag-end. "Tag-end" scants the reality and those who live it. Mary has lived with dementia for nine years since her diagnosis, and for who knows how many years before that—three or four for sure, maybe many more. Twelve years at a minimum, say. As long as her school years, kindergarten to Grade 12.

As long as having her five children, until my youngest sister was almost in kindergarten and I was about to enter high school. As long as growing up, then.

A seventh of her life, let's say. And a fifth of mine, beside her.

A big, big part of life; and as real as any other. Filled with momentous changes, close-grained with challenge and response, crowded with new relationships. In short, a lived life.

That life is what can never be conveyed by statistics or by case studies in deprivation.

~

I want to tell you in these pages of some of the wholly unexpected riches Mary found in the cave of dementia. How she brought them out to glitter in the sun.

I told her, years ago (and I hope not just this once): I admire you more than I can say, and couldn't be prouder of what you have accomplished.

Unused to praise, she shot me a timid glance and bowed her head. I believe in that moment she understood.

Knowing what you're embarked on, I can wish for you nothing higher than that you have some moments such as these. And that you share them with your loved one.

Speak them. Give them voice. It's what you have most definitely.

I would have done anything I could have done to have spared her this. But, since it had to be, it's been my privilege to have gone through it by her side. I wouldn't have missed it for the world.

~

Look at the person with dementia before you. See them with honest, open eyes. (It's not easy to do, but no harder than it is to do with anyone else.) See them plainly for the warrior they are. Meeting terrors you can't imagine, and can't try to without a shudder.

And meeting them not only with heart-stopping fortitude, but with a resourcefulness impossible to comprehend.

The bravest, most persevering person you'll meet today? There's a good chance he's trying to dress himself, or tackling the dilemma of a meal. Sitting in a chair surrounded by strangeness, or making her slow way down a hall.

~

None of this—does it need to be said?—is to deny the ravages, the sheer devastation of dementia. That would be impossible to do, and grotesque to try. It is only to correct in a modest way an imbalance. For every thousand pages describing how living is shattered by this dread disease, there should be at least one page observing how living goes on within it, and even—approaching this with all due caution—is, in ways, at moments, enhanced by it.

~

Am I up to this? Me? You know best why you ask. Accosted for years by a sense of deep inadequacy, you feel now a preposterousness in your role. Help her? Help him? It's been all I can do, and very often more than I can do, to help myself.

You often find the very sick among the ranks of caregivers. Full-time helpers who are themselves cancer patients, heart sufferers, copers with canes and braces, soldiers of depression, pre- and post-psychotics, disability pensioners, the frail, the elderly... Why us? they may well ask. Why me?

Not from an unwillingness to give care, but from a disbelief that they can. Not *why*, but *how*. How on earth?

I know that *how* well. I've lived inside it like a burrow. My nest of broken twigs. Of soft, twined cast-offs.

Including those two years in hospital, between the ages of twenty-two and forty I spent seven years entirely disabled—unable to work, often unable to leave my bed. Other crises and periods of impairment stretch before and after those, forcing all manner of cutbacks and curtailments. Changes of plan, foreclosures of hope. Bad health is my oldest adversary—and my oldest ally. Other-self, evil twin, enemy…friend?

And you? You know your own mischance. That faulty, misshapen story arc you struggle to smooth out, conceal, edit, mute.

You give care from your strength, a strength informed by weakness. A strength that *knows*. Respect your frailty if you can't yet love it: it taught you to be tough. It cracked you open. And what good ever flowed from a sealed container?

~

You will meet disaster birds. These soar, shrieking, far above the carnage on the ground, which they see as abstract shapes

called Realism, Practical Necessity, Biology,
God's Will, Destiny. Their cries, wind-bent,
will tell you disaster is not terrible but only a
fact. Or not terrible but a gift.

Here on the ground it is terrible. And a
fact. And, sometimes, a gift.

Dear ——

Be with.

(The shortest thing I have to write to you also
happens to be the most important.)

Decisions will come easier, and you'll beat yourself up less, if you remember that, at every stage, being with the person you're caring for is the best way of caring for them.

Arranging for medical attention, monitoring nutrition, hiring extra help, managing legal and financial affairs, talking to health care workers, buying clothes/drugs/toiletries/snacks, doing laundry—all these matter. A lot.

All of the dozens of things you do for your loved one matter a lot.

Being with matters more.

What will we say if someone on their deathbed says, *I missed you?* Will we answer that we were busy balancing their accounts, consulting with their carers, and organizing their affairs?

I missed *you*.

Being with won't always mean being physically with. Phone calls, letters, deliveries of flowers have their place, as does backing off sometimes. Thoughtful absence is the white space, or ground, from which the figure of presence appears. Thinking of someone with fondness, with concern, is also an important way of being with. It conditions the heart to kindness.

But being with in person trumps all else. It's the one way of caring most likely to be right, and least likely to be regretted.

We are animals, evolved to live in small groups. Our big brains, which roam beyond the time and space of our bodies, allow us to extrapolate someone's actual presence from tokens of their presence (cards and flowers) —but why should we make the dying extrapolate us from our gestures?

Don't they deserve our presence and our time? Have we anything better to give?

The answer is obvious, and resonates through the smallest moments.

We have nothing better, and very little other, to give than our presence and our time.

All our other decisions and actions might be delegated to another. Only these never can be.

How do we care for each other in our time of greatest need?

Luckily for us, the simplest way is the best way.

Be with.

Really, is there anything better you have to do?

~

Mary's first home as a person with dementia was a retirement residence, a common first stop. Dementia makes a class of refugees, forever on the run, forever seeking safe haven from a tyrant that won't let them be. The pursuer within keeps narrowing your options, backing you into a tighter and tighter corner. A small suite of rooms in a supervised building. A room and bathroom in a building with more supervision. A room on a locked floor. A bed.

A retreat under fire, I've often read, is the most difficult of military manoeuvres. You no longer hope to win, but bend all your efforts to forestall a rout; and you do so with dwindling resources and morale, foremost your own. Sometimes the retreat under fire is called a withdrawal under fire. (It is the "under fire" part that doesn't change.)

Dementia is a retreat under fire. Caring for someone with dementia is a retreat under fire.

~

No stone unturned says the motto on the School of Retreats Under Fire. Only the still advancing can afford the dream of carelessness.

~

The first weeks and months of caregiving are apt to be remembered as the time of decisions. There aren't more decisions than at later times, there may in fact be fewer, but you're not yet used to making them for another person, especially not for such high stakes.

It comes more naturally to parents perhaps. They're used to pulling the strings for someone else. But even they must feel a wrench at pulling the strings for a much older person. Doubly so when the person is their own parent, which seems to reverse the natural order of things. (It doesn't, it only reveals the order in its full reversive arc: from dependence to independence, then back to dependence.)

Like anyone with new responsibilities, and anxious to fulfil them well, the new caregiver attends to each task exactly, sometimes with uneasy intimations of a deeper duty that is being slighted, but too afraid of error to depart from strict form.

As a consequence, safety and physical well-being and administrative detail all get handled far more minutely than the more looming but more nebulous concerns of heart and mind.

We cling at first to the letter of care, deferring and, at times, forgetting its spirit.

We behave like the young parent who arranges the child's safe drive to school, packs her lunch, dresses her warmly, tops up school supplies, reviews progress reports, meets with teachers, etc., but who, in the course of doing all that, skimps on just sitting beside the child and listening to stories of recess, or snuggling to banish a bully's hissed remark.

This is not to equate dementia's "second childhood", its sometimes childlike echoes, with childhood. They're not the same, despite evocative overlaps, and the impulse to indulge an easy analogy has to be resisted. It disserves both childhood and old age.

~

When I signed the papers to move Mary into Belleview, Ian, the general manager, said to me, "You know this won't be the last place she lives." His saying so was not part of the legal contract; but informally, I think, it was. Professionally or personally, or both, he had to clear the table of illusions. Yes, I told him. Did I know? I did and I didn't. If anyone had asked, I could have said that Alzheimer's was a progressive, untreatable and invariably fatal disease; that, if Mary lived long enough, she would experience growing incapacity not just in memory but in all areas—but that's the knowledge of "and so forth" and "et cetera". It can be hard-headed, it can be terrible; any prognosis can rhyme off all the worsts. It isn't lived yet.

~

The person with dementia is moving in stages from an independent life to a life of total dependence. But the dependent life has been there from the start, and the independent life is still there, flickeringly, at the end, mingling in proportions that change overall and also from moment to moment. Which life am I addressing, which life most needs honouring now—the questions complicate every exchange, every decision.

Belleview, in Dundas, was the retirement residence Mary and Bill had chosen to live in, if they had to live somewhere other than their home. It was a decision reached with difficulty, over many halting conversations. I urged them to make it, and I don't know how real it ever was to them. I sometimes had the sense that they were talking about it, visiting the occasional retirement community, making a list of ranked choices, because that is what you do when you're in your eighties. What you're supposed to do, if you're responsible. If you're realistic.

However the decision was made, it was Bill's decision mainly. Mary went along. But now he was gone, and she still had to live somewhere. Or he was going—it was mid-July and he had less than a month to live—and she would have to live somewhere afterwards. With us? No matter how many times I ran through it, imagining it from different angles, I couldn't make it work. (Here I need to sketch a little my home life.) Two people with bipolar illness, out all day at low-wage jobs; someone with dementia, who cannot safely be left alone night or day; our fourth-floor apartment, appliances, a big, strange city—I kept juggling these facts, adding in the money Mary had available (a new apartment? hired help?), and at times saw ways it might work, but, in the end, I couldn't find any way even remotely likely to preserve my sanity, or my wife's, or our jobs, or our marriage. *And then what good will I be to her?*

And how long might she live? Bill's last illness was a month's crisis—at his bedside, barely sleeping. But what if the month becomes a year? Many years? Not a crisis, but a life. How does a crisis become a life? How is it *lived*?

My thoughts, if they were thoughts, dashed between one big *must*: take her in, keep her safe, help her in her dark—and one big *must not*: go mad, break apart, lose health/job/life... *And then what good will I—*

Caregiving performs every day this two-step of the possible: what is—*what should be*—can't be—*must be.*

~

Because you're speaking for. As. POA = Power of Articulation.

~

She wanted to go on living in the townhouse. If she couldn't do that, she wanted to live in Belleview, as they'd decided. She went back and forth, and elsewhere. She was eighty-four, her husband was dying, she had Alzheimer's. She came with me to Belleview, liked it still, liked it again, wanted to "go there". You can assume at any time that someone with dementia is making an informed decision, and when the decision is convenient it is a tempting time to do so.

And maybe—could it be—you're not wrong? She was running her life, managing it, last year, last month, yesterday—in large measure, in part, sort of. There is a sliding scale. There is a sliding. This person asking about mealtimes, inspecting the carpet—she looks, acts, as she always did, doesn't she? We're not at radical rupture yet. Not at past-the-point. Like that cottage comedy she always relished: the boat drifting away from the dock, someone on the boat tugging a straddler in, someone on the dock tugging the straddler back; the straddler wanting to jump in, wanting to jump back; some moments when the boat might be brought back, so the embarking or disembarking can be tried again, done properly—she always laughed loudest when the conclusion was watery. "Into the drink," she'd chortle. "Right into the drink."

~

I wasn't used to being someone's POA. Wasn't used to what that means. She was my charge, my responsibility. She was also my mother. Mary. Herself. At times, back then, she still looked in control, in charge. (At moments even now she seems so.)

The truth is, there's no graceful way to take control of someone's life away from them. Their driver's licence, their banking, their choice of where to live and whom to live with. What to do, and when. The lifetime habit of turning to and asking, What would you like, is a hard habit to break, and a terrible one to succeed in breaking.

Caregivers, even of those in coma, go on talking to them, asking their opinions, asking their preferences—of course they do. In Bill's last days of unbroken sleep, I talked to him as much as or more than on any days of our lives. Errors creep in from wanting to let the dying keep what's theirs, but no one wants to be in the hands of someone incapable of such errors.

~

Erring humanely, erring on the side of autonomy over safety, hope over expectation —but erring.

I told Bill once, when he was asking me about my priorities as their POA—he and Mary sitting across from me in the living room, Bill doing the asking, Mary just watching and listening—that I wouldn't hesitate to make the hard call (*to pull the plug*), but I wouldn't do it easily. But, of course, to not do it easily is, inevitably, to hesitate.

~

So how, if errors are endemic, do you make peace with making so many of them? How do you live with getting so wrong, so often, what you so badly want and need to get right?

I don't know. I wrestle with it every day. Partly it is about redefining what error means. Though "redefining" sounds too intellectual, too authoritative. It feels more like sifting errors after they come to light, feeling their weight, feeling their source to find which ones were made with heart, from love—and which ones weren't. Or probably weren't, or weren't enough. It's the opposite of hard science, but it's not soft art either. It's Self-Assessment in Natural Light—a portrait needing art and science.

Errors made with heart, from love—these can be regretted but should never be deplored. Wouldn't you be content—wouldn't you feel blessed—if the only mistakes people made with you from now on were made from love of you, from an ardent wish for your well-being? Wouldn't you accept—being the messily complex and constantly changing creature that you are—that even people with those impeccable motivations would often miss the mark? (You, after all, living at Self Central, miss it constantly.)

~

And the other kinds of errors? The ones made, not from love, but from things much less warmly fuzzy. Inattention, sloth, resentment, anger…add your own flaw—it's a big, jostling line.

Hey, you're only human. Don't beat yourself up. You'll hear it from others, you'll hear it from yourself. But does it scan? Maybe, after serious and avoidable screw-ups, a self-respecting human deserves a moderate beating. Self-administered, of course, and not vindictively or cruelly prolonged. If everything glides smoothly into an endlessly forgivable past, what sticks around vividly enough to reform the present?

Beware of the temporal mission-creep by which self-forgiveness morphs into self-licence. Forgiveness follows fault ever more promptly, until one day it precedes it.

Also, *only human*—what does it mean? Human like an axe murderer? Like a Red Cross volunteer? Like an axe-murdering volunteer? Playing the species card can only bring you, via a vast lazy circle of possibility, back to the one human being you've actually been. Better to arrive there sooner.

Don't ask the moon of yourself. Really? Of whom then (the moon-shot being needed)?

Ask the moon; your loved one deserves it. But forgive yourself—after many valiant tussles with gravity, after many hope-surpassing flights—for being, finally, that earthbound human.

~

Belleview was wrong for Mary in many ways. It asked for too much independence, and it imposed far too much solitude on someone in grief, in dementia, living alone for the first time in her life. Saying that, though, I still don't know if it was a wrong that could have been avoided or simply one that had to be lived through. Dementia is a going from one wrong or sort-of-right to the next. How could it be otherwise? Where is the perfect home when your brain is being dismantled?

Still, I deluded myself sometimes. A pure intensity of wishing overpowering the facts. Watching her make her way into the dining room packed with other seniors, praying she will make new friends, sick with fear that she won't (like—the analogy whispers—a parent watching a child take uncertain steps into a new schoolyard)—*may be* and *must be* obscure *what is*.

~

Errors are as personal as fingerprints. But some of what led me astray may lead you, too.

I didn't know enough about dementia. You never do, since dementia is always changing. Every decision is on the fly and inexact and behind the moment. (Which is still better than ahead. Behind accepts risk as the price of possibility. Ahead is safe, but restrictive.)

I tried to make caregiving *one more* thing I was doing, fitting it in on top of everything else: day job, executing Bill's estate, managing mental illness—it was far too much. Caregiving is too big. If you're determined to do it well, you've got to off-load elsewhere. I skimped on mental health. Skimped on health, period. Sometimes I'd catch sight of a wan, eroded figure slouching in a public space, and think, "Ah, the poor old bastard," in the instants before recognizing myself.

Not all of that was avoidable—caregiving grinds down—but some of it was. I could have hired an executor. I could have hired myself—as executor, as caregiver—and reduced my day-job hours. I could have hired, as I later did hire, helpers. In short, I could have treated myself with half the consideration I would treat a stranger collapsing under multiple heavy loads.

I was deluded about how much my siblings would help. I hoped for, and laboured to arrange, a rally round, a team lift. I got something far closer to a solo hoist. (Far from unusual in caregiving, as I learned. I hope you are the exception.)

I was too in thrall to Mary's lifelong fondness for "nice" homes to see that what she needed above all, niceness be damned, was a home where she was surrounded by love.

I got things right, too. Lots of them. And you will too.

You can up your percentage of them by making, and revising often, the most accurate inventory you can of your own resources.

~

What have you got that you can draw on? Honestly. Don't try to wow anyone (including yourself). Don't undersell either (ditto).

How much money? If you've got it, spend it. Buy time, buy space, buy equipment, buy helpers. *Don't throw money at the problem*, people say. Wrong. Throw it. But *at* the problem. And, obviously, don't throw more than you have.

How much room is in your own heart? What a piercing, intimate question! But there's no way, finally, to avoid its intimacy or its piercing. Caregiving is going to take your measure as a carer. It is going to pace off, again and again, the dimensions you allow another to occupy in your life. Your heart will be rated as a landlord. The more honest a rating you can make yourself, the less likely you are to advertise space you don't have, or to call top-quality a space that turns out to be a slum.

More prosaically, what about your health? Your time? Caregiving places gruelling demands on health, jobs, relationships, all other interests. Often it dissolves or wrecks them. Anything felt to be expendable, friends and hobbies for instance, usually disappears early on. Perhaps to return later, perhaps not. Caregivers are chronically underslept, overworked, ill. Often they are very sick, and sometimes they are dying, following a pin-step behind their loved one.

How stretched thin are you at the outset?

No, really. How thin?

~

Another way of asking this is: How many persons with dementia are in the room?

Sleeping so little, keeping so much in your head, your thoughts are often confused and scattered. Or they are focused laser-like on the current crisis, blinding you to all else.

Dragging so much grief around, you journey deeper and deeper into a sadness at what is happening, a sadness at the way things are. It colours what you see, it stops you from seeing more. You feel autumnal, you feel shadowy. You become both dense and faint. This is sadness as a way of life. This is dying as the communicable disease it is.

You are isolated. You've stopped seeing friends. They know nothing of this life, and you know nothing else. Your pastimes together are just that: past times. Everything that can be thrown from the lifeboat must be.

Your other pastimes, too. The things you used to enjoy doing—they are expendable, they get pitched. (But these things that consume too many hours and minutes are also, and have always been, your story. They are you.)

You're sick. A little or a lot, on multiple fronts. Almost as if you've forgotten how to be a body. Poor sleeps, bad appetite and digestion, skin eruptions, joint and muscle pain. Any pre-existing conditions you had are worse. You look frailer, paler, and a lot older, suddenly.

Sleep-deprived (unwell generally), confused, grieving, alone, your story gone— you know now why depression is a pseudo- dementia (it is only the *pseudo-* part you doubt).

And so you turn to, you spend even more time with, the one best placed to understand. The one who is also, along with you, in dementia.

~

And yet, despite the constant time together, you often lose sight of the person you are caring for. It is a paradox that underlies all care.

The drive to know someone well enough to care for them obscures as it reveals.

Amassing particulars from close up, you lose the larger view. Attending to what is wrong, you forget the much that is right. Gaining certainty, you erode mystery. Learning to answer confidently, you forget to question humbly. Enjoined to act, you neglect to sit and wait.

Caregiving builds up an encyclopedia of knowledge about the other, but its obverse is always a larger ignorance. You have always to stand a little in awe of the one you are caring for. Awe at the magnitude of what they're facing, only a little of which you can comprehend. Awe at the numberless means by which they face it, only a few of which you'll ever see.

Mostly, the intense focus of caregiving is its own kind of obliviousness: putting all you've got into each tiny movement, like a rock climber, you learn minutely what is right in front of you, without seeing very far up or down.

You peer less at what's up ahead. Which in very many instances is no small mercy.

Unless, of course, what you want to peer at is the person you're caring for.

~

Crawling along on a sometimes two-hour commute, micro-comas in a fog of exhaust and brake lights, I felt a physical dread of dementia, busy far up the road, easily out-running this limping care. But what of Mary herself? She is easy to lose sight of. Easy to displace from the centre of her story: sad, confused, frightened, mostly alone. Con-fronted at every turn with appalling new realities, fighting them in every way she can.

In the seventeen months I was struggling to learn to be her caregiver, she was journey-ing, far more momentously, seventeen months deeper into dementia itself. Many hells are darkest nearer their starts, when memories of the former life attack most sharply. When large parts of the abandoned self still linger on a visible shore, bereft and calling helplessly for your return.

Mary was a Depression-era farm girl from Saskatchewan, a Sick Kids nurse, a mother of five. By temperament and life experience she is averse to calling attention to her own pain.

But not even a lifetime's quiet arts of forbearance could hide the deep darkness of the hell she was in.

~

An evening.

Some time in the fall of 2011. Probably a Friday, because it's easiest for me to get off work early that day, and it's still light out.

Mary opens her door, beaming welcome. ("Mary's smile", pronounced as a force almost apart from her, is something everyone she meets remarks on.) She's so happy to see me, she says.

Unjust though it would be, I keep expecting her to blame me for the loss, within a few short weeks, of her husband, her house, her way of life, and, with rare exceptions, any other visitors. It would make sense to blame. Who but a bad guy could wreak such harm? But she never does, not once.

We eat our takeout Chinese. She says the "little chickens" (chicken balls) are good.

From time to time, she hums or sings a few bars along with her Gershwin CD.

When she dances in the narrow space, her face has the bemused, slightly frowning look it gets when she is trying to find a way to move around the pain in her knees and hips. Tonight she settles on a kind of swaying in place, with languid hand-twirls like a slowed-down Bollywood.

She likes the light of her lamp reflected in the window after it becomes dark, she keeps turning to look at it. Finally she asks me what house it comes from.

~

Years after visiting me when I was at my sickest, people said in marvelling tones: *But you laughed, you even joked sometimes.*

Yes, I did those too.

Hell as an address—absolute as Heaven —is not the hell you live in.

Not every evening was so placid, to be sure. But I always drove away from seeing her less frightened than when I arrived.

~

In purely physical terms, Mary looked better after a couple of months at Belleview than she had in two or three years. Perhaps better than in several years. Anxious at entering the dining room alone, she was skipping many meals. Still, she put on weight. I'd arranged a weekly hair appointment for her in the first-floor salon. We did her laundry together. The difference made by these basic interventions told me, better than I thought I'd known, how low her self-care had sunk during the past few years when she and Bill had been struggling along in the townhouse.

It also suggested how far she'd already travelled, secretly, into dementia. (Which by extension implied how far this semi-independence was from where she needed to be.)

The phone and TV were a nightmare. I taped many How To Use signs to each, simpler and simpler each time. Yet often she couldn't get the TV turned on, or get a shrieking channel turned down or off. The phone sometimes connected her to me, but often to misdialled strangers, some of whom contacted me to claim the money she'd promised them.

The shower was another minefield. She'd always taken baths. Now she had to contend with a dial with coloured markings, a tandem of levers, a safety chair. The forcefulness of the jetting water frightened her, as did the tall, three-sided alcove, a tiled cage with the curtain closed.

I showed her, several times, how it worked. Later, toward the end of her time there, community care workers came to try to help her. Sometimes she let them, sometimes not.

In the year or so between, I'm ashamed to say, I can't be sure she had more than a handful of showers. Or how she might have been keeping herself clean otherwise.

It seems like I should remember more. But nothing else is coming back.

Is it possible basic hygiene fell through the cracks? Could I have let that happen?

Along with what else?

~

She spoke to me of "people going in the factory". Looking out of her window, I saw a shed-like building across the street. And children going down a lane behind it to reach an unseen school. When I squinted I could compress the two scenes into one, as she had, involuntarily it seemed. (She seemed not to see a difference between the children and equally sized, more distant adults.)

It was a bit like her old whimsy, but darker and more confused. It seemed like whimsy and dementia collaborating. Imagination one more thing for dementia to work with, and on.

~

The story of Mary's life was simplifying on its way to breaking down. Simplifying as a way of breaking down, and as a way of managing breaking down. For everyone, there will always be a story. As caregivers, our job is to try to hear it. What it is and what it is becoming.

A simpler story: a retreat under fire.

Story first. Story above all.

~

Like all robustly imaginative people, Mary had always struggled with the transition between sleep and waking. It wasn't just that she was a grumpy riser, muttering to herself as she got breakfast going. She had trouble coming from the dream world all the way out into waking life. She blended the different realms into a hybrid. A patchwork fantasy that dispersed far more slowly, and far less conclusively, than it does for most people.

It was a lifelong problem. And related in some complicated way to her down times, "away" spells ("oh…just thinking"), and to the drinking problem she developed in her fifties and which continued, through various reforms and fallbacks, until her eighties. Until her Alzheimer's, in fact.

Did dementia in some way take the place of alcohol? A new airlock between dream and waking?

(Conjecture is crude but unavoidable. At least for a story you care about. You jot notes. You draw bare diagrams.)

~

Wild, glaring eyes, a panic in her face, tears sometimes—these were signs that she was trapped in the zone between dream and waking. Unable to get back, unable to get fully clear.

We argued then. Then, especially. Nagging cycles of call and response that circled a grievance perseveringly. Why did I think she'd lost the money? Why wouldn't I give her more? Why couldn't she go home? Why couldn't she go back to Saskatchewan on the bus? These ended, since she didn't tire, only when I turned away. Sometimes I had to physically remove myself—come back twenty minutes later and begin the visit again. She would beam a smile of renewed—or brand new—welcome.

We didn't argue often, really. But we'd hardly argued at all before. Sometimes I was heartened by our new ability to let off steam, ease the pressure cooker we were in together.

Her new readiness to fight seemed part of a new emotional openness, generally. It wasn't just anger she expressed with a new plainness. An undemonstrative person all her life, she now gave voice unequivocally to love, to gratitude, to need, to loneliness. To all the ways she felt.

There was no ducking, no faux-eloquence. *I love you. I don't know what I'd do without you. I'm sad.* (Or: *Mary's sad. She's sad.*—Signs of things to come.) *I'm lonely. I need people.* (Hard to hear, in the last, precisely what was being said, and I missed its full meaning for a time. I need people, not like wish-I-had-more, but like oxygen, like water.)

She hugged, and hugged back, more naturally than ever before. No tentative, formal distance observed. No shrinking or stiffening if it went on too long. She grabbed and held.

All in all, there seemed a new purity to her feelings, as if they were finally peeping out clear from behind the cloud bank of cognition, now dissipating, that had hidden them for a lifetime.

I hardly thought, of course, that dementia was a good trade for this opening-up. But it couldn't be denied that they were both happening at the same time. And it made me wonder about the sheer level of "smarts" required to keep us from ourselves.

~

Other times, more frequent really, a sweetness coloured the story she was making. Listening, I felt I was in a meandering book of tales, which must have reawakened on some level stories she had once read or made in my hearing.

As she roamed through her life, favouring more and more the distant past, I could hear the burnished capitals in her voice: Father—Mother—The Farm—My Brothers and Sisters…like chapters of her life, the first and firmest life, she was wandering through. The Greens, the Farm. Mary Barnes? Mary Green.

Green, the colour of new growth. Green, the colour of prevailing.

Sometimes I could see a fantasy growing, in a plant-like way, becoming fact from one visit to the next. Sometimes even within a visit. *My Father was a nice man. Ster… stork… Strict?* (laughs at herself) *Yes, strict sometimes. Like You.*

My Father and You. You, my Father. Are you my Father? In the next home, she would ask this often.

~

A musing manner like a veil thrown over seriousness helped her build a new story out of fragments. A bluff assertion of the outlandish, a decided step over the line, a stepping stone to get where you need to be. *You were always a good Brother.*

Going deeper into story. Making whatever story is possible. Making of the possible your story.

~

Like a veteran cook making soup from odds and ends, half-rotted scraps, she decocted story from a dwindling store of people, places and things. Long-simmered nouns; a thin, savoury tale.

It was a parsimony I related in part to her upbringing in hard times on the farm.

A Depression-era child (born 1926), she was schooled in privation. Those years met, and helped to make, a native storyteller. Helped to fashion or confirm a willingness to settle for less, a determination to be glad of it. Glad is the stronger storyline.

That proud relinquishing infused the stories she'd always told of life in the Thirties on the farm in Boharm, Saskatchewan. Her father (Strict, Nice) bringing home a chocolate bar, cutting it into seven equal bites for them. Mother (Patient, Nice) sitting late at night under a lamp, unstitching a sister's dress to refashion it for another. Happy Days, she said.

(Though in 1945, a year after high-school graduation, she took the train alone east to Toronto to become a nurse.)

~

"I'm a lucky girl," she said sometimes at Belleview. Occasionally at first, then more often. It frightened me a little. I thought she might be telling it to herself to try to believe it. Later, I realized she was achieving the belief. Achieving made belief a fact. That helped me achieve it too.

~

Mary's friendliness to spiders was a thing that amazed and frightened people all her life. They would watch, wincing, as she held out a hand to let a spider climb onto it, then turned her hand calmly back and forth as it walked or ran about, before setting it back down. Once in a while, the spider bit—*Ow*, she said, *Ow*—and she set it down more quickly, but didn't slap or shake it off. Watching this, even as a child, I had the sense of a strong and independent spirit it would be wrong to confine inside the simple palindrome *mom*.

~

Some time that first fall, I started getting calls. Sometimes one, two in a week. Sometimes not for a couple of weeks. A month, even. Then the phone would ring again.

At any time of night or day—three a.m. the same as three p.m. I jumped at the sound, my heart thudding. Her voice was at the other end, hollow as a Mayday routed from Pluto:

Where am I?

What do I do?

Where is everybody?

There was no hiding from the questions. They meant exactly what they said. Primal questions. What you ask when existence itself, the self existing, is dissolving.

I hung up and drove over. Or I talked her down. Or talked her down by promising to drive over.

I realized at some point that, given her difficulty with the phone, I was getting only some of the calls. Maybe only a small fraction of them. I'd seen her, in our phone training sessions, dial and dial again the number on the card I'd printed, getting a wrong number, getting nobody.

How often, dialling from hell, did she get a stranger or a dial tone?

~

Where am I? What do I do?

The sound of hitting bottom, finding absolute zero, couldn't be clearer.

She was there. We were there.

I didn't have a clue what to do about it.

Was there anything to be done about it?

Except—be with. Be more with.

Be with be with—that broken, blessed record.

~

There was a double line of photographs that I came to hate and fear. It was one of the first things I put up at Belleview, in the short hallway between her room and the bathroom and entrance alcove. They were photographs, taken at ten-year intervals, of her five children. I was twenty-one in my later photo, eleven in the one underneath it; my youngest sister, twelve and two in her pairings; my other sister and two brothers ranged between.

Mary would look at these sometimes and ask me, "Where are they? Why don't they come?"

She didn't ask it often, and never with an edge of accusation or grievance. That made the question worse. It carried no overtones of axe-grinding I could sharpen or try to blunt.

It was, horribly, an honest question.

Which only for one picture could I answer. *Sue, your second child, lives overseas. She'll see you for two weeks on her vacation. (She'll move back, two years from now. We'll become a family of three.)* For the rest, I had no clue. I murmured evasions I hated and don't regret.

It is a common story. Near-universal, from what I've seen. In corridors and day rooms, caregivers trade stories of the "absent ones", taking from them a bitter strength.

Cold affirms the building of fires. Absence gives presence its sturdy shape.

Mary grieved the loss of her children. Said their names while she remembered them. But I never heard her blame. Not them, not me, not herself, not her condition. She isn't a saint. In her healthy days she played favourites, suffered jealousy and fomented it, carved as many closed circles as anyone. Which made her achievement now of simple grief all the more remarkable.

They were gone. They weren't with her. She was sad. It seemed as pure as that.

And that, at least, seemed admirable. Seemed to me—reeling with pity and rage that I only effortfully brought under control —almost beyond belief.

Far along in dementia, she was teaching me things. Things I might never be able to learn in a more than rudimentary way. But things of inestimable value nonetheless.

~

Reading was another loved thing she gave up only with great resistance, and also without blame. Never needing to turn her love to hate to let it go.

(Even now, nine years into dementia, she clings to a vestige of reading, piecing out her surround of letters. "Nik-res": Snickers. "Bur-daw": Birthday. "Frill": Fire Drill.)

She used to sacrifice half a night of sleep just to finish the latest Taylor Caldwell or Joyce Carol Oates (weird, she called the latter, but kept reading her). If I got up in the middle of the night there was a better than even chance she would be sitting in the armchair in the living room, head down in the lamplight, smoke from her cigarette curling above the pages.

She kept some books around her at Belle-view. They continued to pull away, keeping more and more of their meaning from her. She kept after them, ungrudgingly. Friends more distant than before, but still friends. Reading a passage three times, six times, a dozen times. Shortening her reading to a paragraph, a sentence. Part of a sentence. A word.

Getting me to read parts out loud. That worked well for a while. The sound of the voice entrancing, even if the meanings hovered for briefer and briefer intervals before disappearing. The voice of the story remained.

She was losing the story she knew. Both of her main stories, which I think at their core were one. The story of books, of literature; the story of stories. The story of family, her family.

Seeing these beloved stories degrade, corrupt, dissolve—un-tell themselves. It has been, perhaps, the sharpest agony of her dementia; perhaps of any dementia. Meaning is oxygen.

And yet keeping her love of each story, and her faith in story itself. In the storytelling that makes story possible, that keeps cycling it up out of chaos, out of nothing.

Losing your story, your place in your story, without losing story.

It was an act of love that pointed far and deep. Pointed to many glowing possibilities.

It dumbfounded and inspired me.

~

More and more, she seemed lost at Belleview. And lost in more and more serious ways. Those phone calls to me. Then those phone calls stopping. She couldn't work the phone any more. Couldn't call out of hell.

At some point she started appearing at the front desk in the middle of the night. In her nightgown, in disarray. Crying, or having cried. *Where am I?* And: *Where are my children?*

Seeming honestly to think she could get an answer. Waiting for one. Delia, at the desk—I used to bring her a doggy bag from our dinner—let me in on these. The times she witnessed, the ones she heard about. I realized I was getting the tip of the iceberg.

I knew these appearances spelled the coming end of her time at Belleview. She would be evicted, though it probably wouldn't be called that.

It's terribly hard to be sure of the timeline of all this. As hard as I try, I can't quite recover it with assurance. As if I was in a dream those seventeen months, a depression, a pseudo-dementia. It's Caregiver Time, another aspect of it. A dimension, a dementia. Shared Un-Time.

Perhaps you already know Un-Time. Perhaps you are reading (as I am writing) to un-do it.

~

Late the next spring, I hired two women —Agnes and Cynthia—to be with her in rotation in the afternoons. They walked together, drove together, sat together. It helped. It reduced hell.

If you can't be with, ask, hire, get another to be with.

It's another, if a lesser, being with.

Don't throw money at the problem. Wrong. Throw the money if you've got it. What else is the damn stuff for? Just make sure you throw it *at* the problem.

I wish I'd thrown even more.

~

Before I end with a final scene, I want to say something that is most important. This letter's frequent focus on missed opportunities and getting things wrong might leave the mistaken impression that I regret Mary's time at Belleview.

In fact I cherish it. It was precious time, time undoing itself almost palpably as it ran. A time when her mind was failing swiftly, and yet she bloomed at times within her loss, like a wheat stalk sprouting through a chain.

My only regret, a deep one, is leaving her alone far too much. I spent a lot of time with her, all I believed I could spare. I should have spent more.

~

I learned *be with* the hard way, from the hardest teacher: *not being with*.

~

Once, I took her to a restaurant where you could sit outside and listen to music. If the weather permitted, I tried to take her out for a meal. Her knees were getting worse, but we could make our way a few blocks to one of several restaurants on the main street.

The weather this day was warm, the evening long, so a spring or summer day, or perhaps early fall—but for the life of me, that caregiver's dementia again, I can't figure out if it was a warm fall day the first year (she moved in at the end of August) or a summer day a whole year later. The latter seems more likely—in my memory we have our routines down, we know where we're going—but if so, her mood, for that later period, seems surprisingly cheerful and relaxed.

Was it so more often than I remember?

We're at a patio table. As usual, she's joking with the waitress. Somewhat awkwardly, saying odd things, but her broad smile carries the moment, as it usually does. (I realize, more and more, that what helps her mourn her lost family is that she finds family everywhere.) The air is mild, twilight long; it must be summer again. As the man behind me starts singing, accompanying himself on an electric keyboard, she orients to the sound with a jerk of her head. As though she's been given a little slap. Instantly she forgets the other people, forgets her food, forgets me across from her. Gazing wide-eyed, with a rapturous smile, she starts moving her body in the chunky, heedless, whole-body loops I associate with blind musicians. It's startling, a little frightening. She looks drugged, all the way into the music, totally unselfconscious. Once again, it seems, she's broken through, surfaced against the steepest odds to possess the moment utterly. She sways even more heavily and eccentrically. Does she just not care how she looks? I think treasonously, glancing around at the patio diners, some of whom indeed are eyeing her curiously. Veering close to tears, I think, I'm glad she reached this point, feeling she must be somewhere near the end (never guessing what now, six years later, still amazes me: how deep into dementia you can go, how much of yourself you can lose, and not only not die but remain, substantially, yourself). I rally then, and see what's right in front of me: this breath-stopping, heart-squeezing, utterly dazzling seizing of pure joy. I feel strong, proud, happy—she lent me these. Looking over my shoulder, I'm prepared to stare down the musician's supercilious amusement.

He, of course, is singing right to her. Playing to the audience of his dreams.

That is the best of it, and it is no small best.

Dear ——

Be with yourself.

If not first, then at least not last. Certainly not
dead last.

~

Airplane survival, people will say to you (you may get sick of hearing it). Save yourself first, or how can you save anyone else?

It's fair advice, but unlikely to be adopted soon by anyone so constituted as to be a long-term caregiver.

You've always been adept at putting others' needs ahead of your own. In the burning airplane, you're more apt to save your seatmate, then the other passengers, then the cabin crew, and then try to settle the screaming pilots—your own self-preservation instincts seeing you no further than the occasional gulp from a dangling oxygen mask as you rush between the smoking, pitching rows...

It isn't pretty. It isn't conducive to a long or easy life. But neither does it make you a monster or a freak.

While you're trying to reform yourself a little—yes, by all means, add that to your list—spare a moment to reflect that there are worse ways to be.

Me first wrecks far more planes and passengers. Perhaps even the one you're in.

~

It's obvious to you by now that this is not the place for exhaustive practical advice on the minutiae of caregiving. What sundowning is and how best to handle it. How to avoid excessive bruising and skin tears. The pros and cons of a mechanical cat. Plenty of that exists—in books and articles, in online posts, most helpfully in tips passed on from other caregivers. Magpie up as much of it as helps. Work up your patch. A good caregiver is a matchless student.

I will be content if, reading these, you feel a little stronger about who you are and what you are doing. About the absolute importance of even the smallest acts of care, and the excellence that adheres to them.

Core strength: the kind you do planking for.

This is meant as planking.

~

There is a message caregivers often get and seldom read. Even more seldom, believe. Almost never remember.

Why not retrieve it tonight from whatever deep pocket or drawer you shoved it in? You still know where—you didn't throw it away, after all. Unfold the torn and grimy slip.

You did good, it says.

And you did.

~

In Oasis, her home for the next thirty-nine months, Mary's battle with dementia became much more visibly pitched. It became violent in the broadest and deepest sense. A last stand (if a last stand can last years).

Ferocious scenes. Harsh measures. Vile encounters.

Screams, yells. Weeping. Curses.

Glaring into the dark, rage smouldering unquenchable.

Torn things. Ripped. Dirty wads. Broken shards. Cuts, unexplained. Bruises. Broken bones. Lesions that don't heal, or heal slowly and regrow. Brown stains on the floor, huge puddles. Abject, exhausted sleeps. Broken things. Broken people.

The list goes on forever, and it did.

I had the appalled sense that Mary was in a cage match with dementia. A contest gladiatorial and to the death, with no tactic disallowed and no quarter given. (*No rest for the wicked*, she used to say, ironing in her kitchen amid the slosh-and-spin of the washing machine, dryer thumps, cries of kids, stovetop sizzlings, and the jiggedy-hiss of the pressure cooker.)

All the ways of hurting and being hurt are one way, which occurs in a dreamtime.

Eating alone in her room on the locked ward two days after assaulting another resident. Flashing out in the hallway to scratch her face and arms. Lying on her bed ten minutes later, smiling a guileless greeting.

Hello. What're you doing?

Oh just. Watching. Watching … the light in my window.

Shrieking on Christmas Eve—*NO! NOOO! STOP! STO-OP! WHAT'RE YOU DOING TO ME? STOP I'LL KILL YOU! STO-O-O-P!*—while the nurse tries to take the sutures out of her face and I try to hold her still, hands on her forehead and shoulder. Rearing in panic at each touch of the tweezers, ripping her own flesh. Because you can't prepare for the next moment if you can't remember the pain of the last. Beaming at me when I return after rinsing the bloody basin. *Oh what a nice surprise.*

Mixed in were times, so many, of sweetness and simple joy. They redeemed the violence, they made it worse. They confirmed nightmare's radical disjunction, the crazed blade still at work amid the talcum and coos of the nursery. You immerse in innocent warmth, share a moment of guileless wonder…and then recall. The phone keeps ringing. You can't wake up.

~

In this time of prolonged demolition, when I could do less and less to help, I realized that my presence was becoming more and more essential. My *role* was diminishing in exactly the proportion that it was becoming a *fact*, a fact of life. I continued to help her in all the ways I had before, but my main role now—the fact I had become—was increasingly to bear witness to what she was going through, to stay close, to be there, a piece of the world that does not change and will not leave, a companion and an emissary from another life, alien and cherished, that was still, at least in this degree of witness, hers.

~

The new phase started with an eviction. Every new phase does. Or an eviction always certifies that the new phase is under way. An eviction moves you to an elsewhere you've already reached. There, an eviction is in progress to a place further on.

Each move—four in seven years, as I said —has come after about a year and a half,

like stages on a journey, a going deeper
into dementia. Each move has been forced:
the place she was leaving never called it an
eviction, but it was always that. "Care needs"
were spoken of—rightly, honestly—but it
was also clear, each time, that she was being
driven from a community. She'd gone further
than the place, and the people in it, could go,
could follow; she had to go elsewhere, be out-
placed. I felt the uprush of fear you feel for
any exile. Going into dementia is a passage of
exquisite vulnerability, and each forced move
sheds another protective layer. Each station
leaves more behind: less safety, less hope,
is carried on to the next leg. We excuse our
exiling by saying it is for the exiles' good—in
part it may be, but it is mostly for ours. We
can't live with them, so we must arrange it so
they do not live with us.

It's not so everywhere, it seems. I read of
a community in Denmark where those in
dementia, with their carers, make and eat
meals together; take forest walks on railed
pathways, the most impaired linked to the rest

by bands, like the bands sometimes linking pre-schoolers on vital but risky outings. The practical humanity of the set-up could make you gasp with longing, make you weep.

But we are not, not yet, in Denmark.

~

Belleview had a floor, their Plus unit, that provided more care and supervision, and there was a Belleview in Toronto, in a part of the city I often worked in. I knew I had to get her to Toronto, where I could visit more. When in doubt, be with. I knew that now. And I still felt, since Mary had the money, that a private home was the way to go, rather than government-subsidized long-term care.

Now, I'm not so sure. Private care homes, like private schools, sometimes offer better services, but they are always overpriced for what they deliver. If you have the means, the best combination is usually a good public facility bolstered by additional purchased support.

But this is the retrospect that tries to idealize a retreat under fire. It pictures the general surveying the terrain and choosing the best from among a range of informed options. In reality, almost every decision is made at speed, with only partial facts, and under severe compulsion.

Make the best decision you can at the time, and try not to look back too critically. If it turns out not to have been good, learn what lessons you can, and remember that you had your reasons for choosing as you did. Rather than fantasizing about the "best" place overall, a better use of your energies is making this place, now, the best place it can be. This is the place, you are the you, you've got. Work with them.

~

Mary's intake interview at the Toronto Belleview was excruciating. Like watching my child (there it is again) sit a cruelly impossible exam. As we were given the tour, I resented (while approving) Mary's pressed clothes, her perm, her good coat brought out of the closet—as if we had to airbrush her for these care providers! But that is the reality of private care. It's a seller's market, and the seller will take you only if you're not too much trouble, and only until you are too much trouble. I seethed while sitting at a table in a sort of boardroom, unable to help as she answered, mostly incorrectly, the questions on her cognitive assessment. When the Director of Care, young, wearing a chic pantsuit, passed Mary a paper and asked her to draw a clock—Mary's clocks, even on a second try, were self-skeweringly small and lopsided, with tiny, scrunched-up numbers placed irregularly around the rim—I felt close to exploding with impotent rage and frustration.

May you get the care you've given was the silent, perfect curse I'd devised early on. It roared in my head in the Belleview boardroom.

Somehow, though, we made it. We got through. The DOC smiled us on: she'd get Mary's records from the other Belleview and be in touch about the next steps. I felt wrung out with relief. It might not be where she needed to be, but since there was no such place (I saw that now), it was *more* where she needed to be. It was a step, we'd work with it. Work on it, work it out.

Two weeks later, the DOC called one morning and said she was denying Mary admission. She was sorry, but she was "too far along…too advanced". Her "care needs couldn't be met".

Whatever I mumbled into the phone—I remember speaking for a time, without any recollection of what I said—I hung up completely flattened. I felt I was on a winter road with Mary, far from one home and another not in sight, night descending, without a clue what to do next.

I was still sitting blankly by the phone when it rang again. It was another woman from the Toronto Belleview. She'd been involved with Mary's tour, knew how disappointed I must be, and wanted to give me the number of Oasis, where she'd worked before.

Just for the suggestion, jogging me out of blankness—since I had no idea what Oasis might be—she was an angel of mercy. You meet them on the caregiving road. They flit down every day.

~

If she was an angel, then Oasis, when I drove up that day to see it, was heaven. It's good, and a little surprising, to remember that now, given the hell Mary went through there. It says something important about the hells of dementia. Maybe about all hells.

Mary's hell was going to happen wherever she was. As far as I can tell, that's true. Some places would make it worse, some would make it better; none would make it disappear. And there's no way of knowing, since I've nothing to compare it with, where Oasis falls on that continuum.

Hell gets measured, in memory, by where you got to rather than by where you started from.

But you lived and made each call not just, not even mostly, from where you got to, but also from your starting point and from every point along the way. It is the nature of hell to obliterate the truth of non-hell. But, in hell above all, you need fidelity to the road.

~

A big, "country-style" house. A rambling farmhouse feel. (*The Farm.*) Christmas decorations. Wooden floors, carpets. Scuffed, comfortable furniture, not oppressively new or gleaming. Smell of cooking. A cat and dog mooching around. Lots of people: residents, staff. Homey.

Faux-homey, sure. A Kentucky private corporation's construct of home. Of course. I wasn't deluded or naïve; merely desperate, with shrewd open eyes. (And with the Mary-eyes I'd grown: internalizing her tastes to choose her home, her furnishings, her clothes, her everything.) Was I going to try to parse the exact difference between faux-home and home? Did I have that luxury? Was I sure there was a difference, or if there was, that I could find it? Find it why?

I need people. Mary had told me that. Told me as often, in as many ways, as she could.

Perfect, I thought, taking it in. Perfect for where she is now. Safe haven reached!

Close call, but made it!

So I thought. A thought like a gasp of relief. And, thinking back on thinking, so I think again.

~

Here in this eddy, where I've fetched up closer to heaven than hell, is a good place to talk about what I found that worked during the Oasis years. I could talk just as honestly about what didn't work, of course. But you will find that out on your own, without anyone's help. Also, in a curious way, the doesn't-work is dumb and inarticulate. It can't speak because it doesn't apply. It doesn't connect.

When you find what works with a person, what helps and almost always helps in their times of direst need, you are close to the essence of that person. You've touched the core of what makes them tick: breath, heart, sustenance, mind.

The list is always short. For Mary, it was and is: Nature (animals, plants, other creatures). Language (stories, voices, other creatures). Company (family, nature, language, other creatures).

Put her in contact with these, as often as possible, and she has a fighting chance to be herself. To be.

~

Find what works with the one you're caring for and you come close to finding them. Finding them at last, or again. And in the process, not uncommonly, finding yourself. At last. Again.

~

Whenever I could direct Mary's attention to a tree, a bird, a squirrel outside her window, her day picked up immediately. Often, it plunged her into a story, which seemed the story of her life, the farmgirl-fantasist, as could happen even indoors, encountering an ant along a table edge, which unleashes a gush of communion: *Well, hello, sir, now just where do you think you're going,. Oh, I know, you're …*

And this urge to contact became far stronger when I could get her outside, to a park or even to a bench beside a tree, and the birds and other animals came close, old friends she could see and almost touch and talk to and be talked to by.

They became even more of a family as she lost, first the names of their differences, and then the differences themselves. Seagulls and geese and sparrows became, over time, "white ones" and "brown ones" and "little ones"—varieties of bird-ness, as they must once have been. As they are.

~

"Look at the. Little ones. Hep. Hall. So happy. Helping. No. *Hopping*. That's it!"

Her eyes never leaving the sparrows hopping on and off the ripped garbage bags. Her face rapt with attention, too enthralled to smile. She has never been more present in her life.

~

Making our inchmeal way around the premises, she teeters from the walker, stoops to peer excitedly. An ant the other day. Tiny transverse traveller. Dark speck crossing our path.

Today this common flower. "Oh pretty pretty yellow. Such a pretty little one."

I see it with her eyes. See it true. Nothing of her sweating, decades-long war on dandelions remains. Hacking, uprooting. Moose maple. Bad grasses.

Finally beyond *weed*.

(*How to get to where you are without being where you are...*

The thought instantly uprooted—but it came.)

~

Language worked in some ways as it had always worked. No longer able to read much in succession—the words increasingly difficult to decipher, and missing their connections with the words that came before—Mary preferred to be read to. I read to her. My sister Sue, who returned from abroad in the summer of the first year at Oasis, read to her. Others occasionally read to her. Whoever was reading, she would lean back in her chair or stretch out on her bed, and, closing her eyes, seem to enter a zone of rich calm, visibly relaxing, lifting clear of anger and sorrow.

She listened to people talk with the same enspelled absorption. They were talking books, just as books were talking people. She herself had always been the largest and most fluent talking book, spilling stories from endless pages. Now, though, there were more gaps in her speech, gaps she couldn't bridge as well with made-up words, or sounds, or quirky faces and gestures. She lapsed more often into sad or surly silence. It was better to hear another talk. That still worked.

~

There is such pathos and nobility in people's fight. Such a terrible dignity in the lengths they'll go to just to go on.

Talking so as not to hear herself think. Talking so as not to hear herself not think.

Losing, moment by moment, battles with despair, without ever finally surrendering to it.

It stops your breath to glimpse it. And then, glimpse by glimpse, gives you new breath to go on.

This privilege, unseverable from its burden, of accompanying.

~

Sue began to visit Mary on Saturday or Sunday. For as long as they were together, I felt the relief I'd known, in the first two years, when Sue flew back from abroad: a bath-like relaxation of body and mind at the thought that Mary had another visitor, her world was richer today by just that much, and that for two or three hours nothing bad could happen to her without my hearing right away.

We texted updates after each visit. Sometimes emailed if there was more to say, with photos or, occasionally, a video. Many texts were about practical matters: things Mary needed, a new health concern, a memo from the staff. Some were about Mary's sadness and distress, or our own.

A surprising number of messages, though —and more as time went on—were about our delight, our repeated astonishment, at the scrappy lastingness of Mary's spirit. That alligator hold on the fullness of her life that she gave up so unwillingly, even in retreat.

They were glimpses of a triumph. Glimpses you share because you don't want the other not to have this miraculous pebble in her pocket, to take out from time to time and roll between thumb and fingertips, marvelling.

Mary's ability to preserve, under such fire, so much of herself stirred us to awed whispers. *Who she was…still.* A deep attainment. But we also felt, though rarely said—it went beyond family news—that in some ways we were seeing Mary as never before. Glimpsing new facets of a person we had known all our lives, and might have deceived ourselves into thinking we had known utterly, but now saw better than before. *Our mother*, yes, but beyond that, this remarkable person. Not a stranger, never. But someone given back—taking back—her rightful power to surprise.

~

It can feel strange to give thanks for what affliction shows you. But stranger still to deny the thanks you feel—why?—to keep your tears pure?

~

To eke out the memory of my ancient cell phone, I began to type out the texts before deleting them. It was extra work I hardly needed, done after midnight, but the further I went alongside Mary into her dementia, the harder I found it to push any sort of Delete button without a back-up. In time, the printed texts, running into the hundreds, made a thick-ish slab in a three-ring binder.

Once—thirty years before—I'd volunteered to type a novel Mary had begun writing. When Bill retired, they each started one. Like most such attempts, theirs petered out. Mary called hers a "saga"—she wouldn't dignify it with *novel*. Its first line has stuck with me: *Don't pick the sea oats.* From a sign she said she kept seeing on their drives through the Carolinas and Florida. The sea oats being the grasses whose roots help hold the sand dunes in place along ocean beaches.

A natural image for Mary to adopt: stalky, tenacious, useful. A transplant from her prairie days.

And, I hope—I would like to believe—a natural image for me as well. What better for a caregiver to be than sea oats: rooting the shifting sands between boardwalk and breakers?

~

As I'd learned in Belleview, Mary would accept pats and hugs as never before. And, as her crisis deepened, she welcomed a new way of being touched, passive and continuous, that might have alarmed her before. What worked, I found, what calmed her best when I answered a distress call from Oasis (Mary long past phoning herself), was putting a hand on her forehead and just leaving it there a while. Putting a hand on her hand, or on her back, the same way. Not moving at all. Just letting her feel you there. Or letting her feel someone, as uninsistent a "you" as possible.

I noticed this with the other residents too, even some of the most withdrawn. Reaching out a hand partway to you, leaning slightly towards, they would request touch. And the touch they seemed most soothed by was the kind that lingered without attempting to resolve the moment. Not a hug, a pat, a hand-shake. They'd take these, if they were what was on offer. But best was just a hand, touching down, resting a while.

All of what works best with Mary—and my main reason for telling it—works best with other residents too. Works in different ways, to different degrees; they are persons with dementia. But works best because it connects with, consoles, ratifies the large domains: Nature. Language. Company. And another, Music. I don't know how I forgot about music since it has been a touchstone of Mary's life, never more so than now. I think perhaps Music, belonging as it does to both Language and Company (and perhaps to Nature too), slipped between them all, present but (fittingly) unseen.

Nature. Language. Company. Music. What are they but a conspectus of communion? Of shared human meaning.

~

Meaning, many would say, is in short supply on a dementia ward. Certainly it often seems so. But the shortage of meaning is not just on the side of the demented. It is on our side too. We, who may mean more as we keep asserting, also mean differently. We demand meaning they can't supply. But they also require meaning we can't supply. And they supply meaning, perhaps in abundance, that we can't recognize because we've never felt the need to ask for it.

The disjunctions feel like different species meeting. The visitor gusting in from outside to give and ask for updates, tick off care concerns; the resident sitting by a window, exploring with fingertips the texture of a cloth. The activity director calling out the names of songs, verses to be skipped; voices rising in halts to meet the tune for a note or phrase, continuing, over awkward jokes, past its end. The time signatures are different, as are the instruments, the keys. It might be Wagner blasting over a bamboo flute. The *New York Times* thumping down on a haiku.

The meagre overlap between domains opens a large, light-filled window on dementia and on caregiving, as an episode from Mary's second home at Oasis illuminates.

~

Oasis moved Mary upstairs to their locked floor, called REM, after fifteen months. Just two months shorter than the time she'd lived at Belleview. These stages happening like clockwork, like something preordained. Fight it with whatever excesses of personal spirit you can summon, they'll be enacted on schedule.

As before, the reasons given for the move revolved around "her escalating care needs". The move was "for her welfare". I don't doubt it. But it's not, and never is, the whole story. I'd been fighting the proposed move for three months, since it had first been mentioned at her one-year care review. Mary was having more trouble with dressing, and with occasional states of partial undress; was needing more care and coaching all round; and was exhibiting "behaviours", which meant arguing with other residents, one in particular, swearing and hitting on a couple of occasions.

These concerned me too, but I didn't think, even in aggregate, they rose to the level of mandating a move that would be, after all, one-way. No one with dementia comes back from a locked floor. You've got to wait until no more waiting's possible. The managers acceded, for now.

They knew, and I knew, that Mary's profile didn't yet stand out markedly from those of the other residents on the first floor, and in fact was milder than some whose families had dug in their heels against a "graduation" upstairs. And I knew, and presumed the managers knew I knew, that we were in the grey zone where care concerns—for these were humane, well-meaning people—shaded into the concerns of corporate profitability. The managers were in a limbo between the front-line care staff and residents and their families, below them, and the director of operations and her distant bosses and their shareholders, above them.

One April evening, during a social function for some of these business people, Mary, whose room was on the ground floor beside the lounge where they were serving drinks and snacks, opened her door in a state of confusion and mild undress. She had taken off her blouse, so was wearing only a bra above the waist. She had been wandering occasionally lately, down hallways mostly without seeking an exit. A PSW would direct her back into her room. That happened now. It didn't seem like anything that should surprise or upset visitors to a dementia care home, especially visitors involved with that business. But the director, hosting the event, felt strongly that a line had been crossed. I couldn't help but wonder if the line was the one where investors in the sausage factory glimpse, inadvertently, how the sausage is being made.

However uncharitable that view may be, the next morning, Mary's move up to REM was presented to us as non-negotiable. No more waiting was possible.

~

Sue and I grieved the move together, it was a terrible day and night—a bunch of terrible days and nights—but we'd fought it off as long as we could. To fight more would mean leaving, and I didn't have another, better place in mind.

Most on the Oasis staff were good, and some were wonderful. Being someone's caregiver stirs up such a helpless stew of feeling, on their behalf and your own, as your twinned orbiting needs whirl through worry, sadness, anger, frustration, fear, remorse. You go through the wringer, day after day, and some caregivers seem to fight with staff and bureaucrats, often spasmodically, in sudden vehement outbursts, mainly to give all that throttled emotion an outlet.

But I think, as a caregiver, you've got to try to get fighting right.

To fight only when, and for as long as, a particular fight serves a purpose. For as long as it holds out promise of helping the one you're fighting for.

Both—all the—ones you're fighting for.

~

A few days after her move up to REM, into a small room at the end of a hall visited day and night by a constant stream of other REM residents we never did succeed in quelling, Mary lurched from her room in the middle of the night and fell heavily, fracturing her pelvis. Before and after her fall, she was heard exclaiming about "children" she had to rescue "from the fire".

Dream. And waking. And dream-waking. And waking-dream. And the slipping currents of meaning that connect them all. This episode was taken as proof that she belonged on REM. And that she needed more, or different, psychiatric drugs than the ones she was already taking. An antidepressant, a sedative, a drug for Alzheimer's—all in mild doses, and none seeming to do much, though how do you tell amid the chaos of dementia?

But wait, I said. And sat some people down. And told them more of what I thought they needed to know about her. She'd worked at Sick Kids. Worked on the burn unit there. The burn unit—fires? Burned children? She

had five children. Most of them she never saw.
They were lost to her—gone. Increasingly,
as she regressed in time, living in her deepest
memories, she saw herself as the young wife,
the young nurse, the young girl she'd been.
She'd just been moved to this locked ward.

Lost children, burned children. Her
responsibility. Save them. It wasn't hard to
see a nexus of meaning here, was it? Tangled
threads meeting in a knot of urgency, of panic.

Mm-hm, people agreed. Doctor, nurse,
social worker. Went on looking at me.

Went ahead with prescribing for her
psychiatric condition.

Did she have a psychiatric condition? She was
terribly depressed, if that is the answer.

(I don't think it's the answer to that particular question.)

But you have a duty as someone's caregiver to intercede not only on behalf of the
meaning they have lost, but also on behalf of
the meaning they have or may have, in the
face of insuperable odds, actually attained.

~

LOFT, a community mental health service called in to assess Mary—who was frailly on her feet again, after several bedridden weeks requiring around-the-clock outside staffing—gets it exactly right with their motto:

All behaviour has meaning.

But LOFT, in its advisory capacity, carries very little weight. It is a little closer than Denmark, while remaining very far away.

~

Meaning attempted, meaning deferred, meaning denied. I want to stick with meaning because I think it provides a key. I think, if we follow it a little further, it may unlock a further room for you. A room where you can function a little more effectively as a caregiver. A room, frankly, if my own experience is a guide, where you can live a little more completely as a person.

How? you ask.

I can only bring back the apple juice of my first letter. Do you remember? The apple juice I found myself actually sipping—that is, sipping and nothing else—when I was a husk, a black wick, in the hospital.

Being is binary, presence rare. You can, on any day, pour something wet and sweet down your throat while you're doing something else. Or you can, once in a magic while, sip apple juice.

The most I can say is that, after these many years of being with Mary, I sip apple juice a little more often.

And—I hope—bring it to others, a little more often, to sit and sip together.

~

Mary began fighting more. Yelling, cursing —at other residents, also at staff. Pushing without warning, reaching out to shove. On occasion scratching, slapping. Whipping her hand out at someone passing in the hall. Once, horribly, punching another old woman she'd knocked down. She hit staff too sometimes, less effectually. No one was hurt lastingly, but there were bruises, sometimes blood. Some of the attacks ended with visits by one or both combatants to the ER.

The incidents happened without warning, at unpredictable intervals. A month would go by quietly. Then things would erupt twice in a week. Or twice in two days. Then quiet, perhaps, for a couple of weeks. Then—

I was dreading the phone more than ever.

Talking to Mary after one of these outbursts, when I'd been summoned and had driven up, I'd find her in her room where she'd been put, her untouched plate of food sitting by (or sometimes spilled on the floor), looking chastened, also ashamed in a vague way, and also, less vaguely, afraid. "Do you remember . . . ?" I'd say, and allude to what had happened.

"No," she'd say, blinking. I never got any sense that she did remember, except as a dark current, a residue of *something bad . . . back there*. "I did?" she'd say, frowning deeply.

There was nothing to be done. You can't counsel what isn't known and can't be recalled.

What may not even ever have entered the conscious mind, except as a whole-body intention, a parcel of dark meaning gathered and pitched, that never needed access to consciousness.

This isn't to excuse, or to explain. I felt awful about the poor old person who'd been hit. I'd catch the eye of their caregiver, if they had one, from half a hallway away, a charged instant in quarantine. Sue had a tense meeting with a victim's relative in the ER, until they saw Mary and the other woman chatting amiably as they waited, giving no hint of the screaming combat that had brought them there.

Each time, I arranged for the seventy-two-hour, around-the-clock supervision by outside Personal Service Workers that Oasis required after a physical assault. I also kept a nighttime PSW on between these monitorings. Mary's care costs climbed to a colossal monthly figure. Four times what they'd been at Belleview, at best. Eight times, at the all-day worst.

What's more, I knew this time I was buying was borrowed. These behaviours put us on the eviction track, just as surely as the distressed nighttime appearances at Belleview had. And I couldn't make up my mind about a long-term-care home to get us on the list. I was visiting them—Sue and I both were—making notes, ranking them, but I couldn't find one that even halfway satisfied me. And fatigue was blotting my will to lurch beyond the status quo.

~

"She's not herself. It's the dementia."

People reach for these kinds of statements, setting-asides. I reached for them myself. It was partly to protect Mary, to protect her view of herself, won and worn through a lifetime. Certainly, battering another helpless old person was an act that would have appalled her, outraging her against herself.

But that raises more questions than it answers about the proportion of unreason in our make-up, and the huge apparatus of cognition it takes to force down the surging impulses that would unseat the person we've built ourselves to be.

A person constructed at least as much by what is not revealed as by what is.

All that ground, again, to make the figure.

She's not herself. Or she's showing more of herself. But, if you show more of yourself, you're not the same self. Less ground, different figure (also a different ground).

The things you growl or scream while driving alone in the car, or say silently in your head the rest of the day, give a sampling of all you have to express but don't (usually). What would people think of you—who would they think you are—if they overheard more of it?

If they saw—if they felt—what you have in you to let out.

~

There is a positive side to this. To the new admission, the new agency, of previously alienated parts. It isn't all roadside ambushes of self and other. Along with accidental ugliness, there is accidental beauty.

Dementia is a story of unravelling. Of dismantling. Of undoing.

Some threads, now undone, will turn out to have been knots that blocked rather than supported, snarls that only looked like ties. Now loosened, now untangled, they stretch to their full length, slender and shining, as they were before the knots.

I put in this category the casual racism that Mary had expressed all her life. Not as insistently or as nastily as many in her generation; her slurs and stereotypes seemed more reflexive, tic-like, though perhaps I am only trying to soften a part of her character I could never view without embarrassment and regret, as well as a little fear, wondering if I could escape this early teaching as thoroughly as I wanted to.

Now, though, in dementia, it was gone. Not just racism, it seemed, but even race-awareness.

She was race-blind (not quite the same as expunging racism, I realize). People were just people, finally. Black, brown, yellow, pink. She oriented to niceness, to warmth—like a sunflower tracking the sun—and had an enhanced ability to detect genuine kindness, as all fragile and dependent persons must. But race, religion, nationality—all that cloud of "ism" and "ity" and "ese"—it was all gone, now. Ballast thrown overboard by the clogged and simplifying brain.

It dissolved in the moment of sinking, leaving not even a silty shadow, like the complexly obscuring but insubstantial murk it might at any previous moment have become.

~

Names were a theme of the Oasis years. What to call herself and what to call the rest of us. Titles had already dropped away (Doctor, Professor, Mrs), roles were slipping and swapping (daughter-mother-sister-grandma), family names were tricksterish (Barnes?

Green?), and given names, though best,
were dissolving. How could she call us, and
herself? What means of address wouldn't
crumble in use, at the touch?

All this while emotional memory was
heightening to a new swiftness and accuracy.

Forget the name of a friend, all right, but
don't forget who is a friend. Or how to scan
a face to see if it spells *friend*. Catch sight
of—burst into a smile with your whole face
at—*friend* shining from the face of the forgotten friend.

This forgetting of names, in favour of a
heightening of the names' meanings, which
had been going on all along, accelerated at
Oasis, especially upstairs in the locked floor
of REM.

It seemed another aspect of war.

It seemed, as well, a bid for peace.

~

The process wasn't orderly, nothing about
dementia is, but through its rapid ebbs

and flows an overall pattern could be discerned. A gradual simplification by which retention of a previous name was struggled for and then discarded. There was a messy logic, but still a logic, to the undoing, with the last-obtained names going first and the earliest names holding out longest. The names fell away in reverse order, roughly, to the order in which they had been acquired.

Mrs Barnes gave way, early on, to *Mary Barnes*. Then, more and more, to *Mary Green*. Then *Mary*. That was bedrock for a long time, and still isn't completely gone. *Mary. I. I, Mary.* It mixed sometimes, then increasingly, with *She. She's hungry. She's tired.* (She had used to say this as a joke, years before. The third person would pop out to make a comic-peevish complaint. *She's had enough, she wants to go to bed.* There it is again, that often uncanny sense that dementia is returning to what was staked out long before, coming back to finally claim it.)

And there was one more name, on a level below this—*you*—but it was only in her next home that she reached it.

~

She asked me, more and more often, who I was. Asked me frankly for my help in placing me. Sometimes, early on, she knew of course. Knew firmly and right away: "Yes, Mike." But often this was coloured with a tone, a pause, of doubt: "Yes... *Mike*."

I am speaking of names here, mainly. I've seldom lost, even now, the sense that she knows who I am essentially: this friend, a tall man with advisory and supervisory capacities (as pertaining to her), some close and abiding connection. She tried to name this, and asked my help in doing so. *Are you my father? My brother? My husband? My grandfather?* My age went wheeling around along with my name. I'd ask her to guess it and she'd say, after a thoughtful scrutiny of my face, *Ninety-one?*

Not how old I feel, I'd think, and remember the times the Oasis staff had mistaken me for a resident, sitting in the row during sing-along or storytime. *How would that work?* I'd say. *You're my mother; you'd be a hundred and twenty*. And she'd throw back her head and laugh.

Age, this farcical thing. She'd speak of herself as a little girl, murmur *Mama*, then look in the mirror, or at her wrinkled arm, and ask who it was. Make a face of disbelief at my answer, or frown or laugh, as at some weird prank.

She tried names and roles for me, as she tried them for herself and everybody else. Settling on one briefly, then moving on. *Mike Barnes. Son, Mike. Bill? My husband. Father. Brother. You.*

~

Here is where many people, even those who may have been on board with caregiving, get off. Does she still remember your name?

People ask me this, fear in their voice. They know that, for themselves, that would be a decisive place to reach. A bridge too far.

A deal-breaker, as we say in these transactional times. The phrase fits the point that many find insupportable: the forgetting by the person with dementia of their, the caregiver's, identity and name.

But it's a hard point for me to speak to, since I don't really share the feeling behind it. Not nearly to the same degree, and often not at all. I'm not sure why. Having lived with serious mental illness for these forty-five years may be part of it; it seems plausible it must be. Having been dismantled and put together—having put myself together—many times. And knowing—learning again and again—the peace of sitting or standing or lying somewhere, without a name or role, but also, at last, without war.

I'm not sure of the reason, and perhaps these cause-and-effect conjectures sell me short.

For whatever reason, when Mary settled finally on "friend" as both my name and role (with, for a time, occasional pop-ups of "Mike")—*Where is my friend?* she would ask the staff, or, at times, *Where is the man?* and then (especially in the next home) *the tall man? the tall guy?*—I felt a peace, a simplicity, and a kind of attainment.

Along with a challenge. Could I be a friend? A man? Stand tall?

~

Stand tall. Be a friend.

To your loved one.
To yourself.
To the next stranger you meet.

What could be harder, or more natural, than that?

Dear ——

I know Alzheimer's will show you terrible things. I hope it may also show you rare and precious ones.

I hope, in the course of taking so much away, it may restore to you your nouns. Place. Person. Thing.

~

Dementia strips you of so much. You the caregiver, along with you the person with dementia. Some of its losses get talked about a lot, but others you hardly ever hear mentioned.

One of these is the *always-have-Paris* delusion. "We'll always have Paris," Rick tells Ilsa at the end of *Casablanca*. And characters in other movies, books and songs tell each other, tell us, that essentials endure. "They Can't Take That Away From Me". "My Heart Will Go On". Culture might almost be described as the *always-have-Paris* industry, so much of it is devoted to the proposition that, come what may, our stories will abide and nourish us.

We say versions of it to each other every day.

It's not true, of course. *Paris, we, us in Paris*: these stories, encoded in delicate, tiny neurons, are more fragile than soap bubbles. Chemical smidgens, the drip of time, bend and deform them. A brief spill of blood can obliterate them. So can a variety of illnesses, so can even common drugs. So can a bang on the head. And so can, so inevitably does, dementia.

Dementia makes clear (its clarifying power is ironic) that every Paris, every we, is a bit of gossamer in the brain, no more guaranteed to stick around than dandelion fluff on a windy day.

And then *we'll always have Paris* seems, not wryly tough (trenchcoats, airfield, night), but naïvely optimistic. Less the wisdom we've earned than the faux-wisdom we've snatched at.

It can wound you, this view. Sap your strength, vampire your vital energies. It can estrange you from your fellow, Paris-banking humans. You can't forget (yet) what they can't remember. Paris can go, Paris is going, all around. You get scared as hell, and sick at heart. Pledging your love, you're sinking in quicksand. You're sinking while brushing your teeth. Where your Picture of Life once hung, this huge panorama in luscious oils, there's an Etch A Sketch dissolving. If only you could return to the innocent days of *Ah, we age and die, but to the end we remember how we lived*.

But *You Can't Go Home Again*.

~

What a downer! Quick, is there a cure?

Yes. I think so. It's simple and extreme (it's a simple and extreme condition). Variably effective.

Always have having gone (it was never really there), you just have now. Paris, brushing your teeth. Paris, looking out on Walmart from the dementia ward. Paris, walking. Paris, driving. Paris in Paris—that, too. The Paris you can find, the Paris you can make. Paris, alone. Paris, together.

Paris, drinking apple juice.

What else is there? What else was there ever?

~

I'll have to make this last letter shorter than the others. I've stolen these four nights from already long days, and I'm tired. Glad, even a little exhilarated, to be writing to you. But tired.

The hours stolen from sleep come after seven years and more of stealing hours.

There are deep arrears.

Caregiving—its small circle, its intensely repeated rituals, its obliterating focus—may seem often to have suspended your life, to have put you in a state of suspended animation from which (you tell yourself) you'll awaken somewhere down the road.

It isn't so, of course. It's another delusion.

You're ageing too, along with your loved one. These are your years. Not an interruption, not a tag-end. For seven years? Nine? Twelve?

A big, big part of life. As long, perhaps, as childhood. As youth or middle age.

Lost friends, lost jobs, lost interests may creep back later. Lost time won't.

This is your time. This is your life.

(Yes, it may scar. Did you hope to be unmarked—by life?)

~

Stillwater, Mary's fourth and current home, felt like breaking through. It felt like finally arriving.

Finally getting to the place that was right, or most right, for her.

I don't think it would have been as right at any time before.

You have your schedule as a care-giver—the best you want for your loved one, the soonest you want it. But dementia has its own schedule. The person with dementia has her schedule. You have to sync as best you can your intentions with what's intended.

I think she got to a place where she could live in a place again, and Stillwater was the place she was living in when she got there.

It helped that Oasis's designation of Mary as "in crisis" bumped her up the CCAC queue, so that we got the long-term-care home at the top of our list.

Help comes in strange forms, at strange times. Shiny bits amid the litter. As a caregiver, you grow bright crow eyes, strong wings and claws, to swoop down and snatch it.

~

Part of the appeal was the name, Stillwater, its pastoral promise. Consciousness of one's subjection to unseen forces compels a belief in magic. All caregivers trust in omens, in auras.

Stillwater calls itself "A Caring Christian Community" and is affiliated with a Pentecostal church. Many people told me that a faith-based home was the way to go, the best bet. However that may be, the ethos of care I largely find at Stillwater doesn't seem to depend, at least not overtly, on religious doctrine. Management may wish you were Saved, but they're not demanding it. There are church services and hymn sings, but no one takes attendance, and no one minds if Mary, or any resident, sings along, chair-dances to, or sleeps throughout.

Still, for me, there is a deeper sense of the pastoral in this building of brick and glass on Sheppard Avenue. It communicates, I can't quite say how, a nearness to rock and grass. To circling, bleating lambs. To wolves. I know it is partly the late stage of dementia Mary is in——but it is more than that. Some kind of clearing has been made, an uncluttering. There is a nakedness to this place.

It drew me, drew my trust, and it continues to. I am not a Believer, but I believe in many things. I practise no Faith, but crave and try for fidelity.

The wide halls, large windows and spare furnishings assist me in this. It is the cleanest of Mary's four homes. It holds to a sense of first and final things.

~

The day we moved her, a cold and rainy day at the end of March, Mary showed no awareness of the change. It was the same when she moved over to Oasis, and when she moved from the first floor up to REM. Not since the move to Belleview, and only a little then, had she registered, by anything she said or did, the fact that she was changing homes. I wondered, again, if she had always been further along in dementia than I knew, or if it meant, or meant as well, that she was resigned to her vulnerability, to having others decide where she would go, what she would do.

This time, I furnished her room far more simply. I put almost all of the pictures, knick-knacks and furniture in storage and waited to see if she would give signs of wanting any of it. She never did. From the start, she seemed calmer with the cleaner lines, bare walls and floors that posed fewer conundrums. She'd always been a diligent housekeeper—she loved cleaning, she used to say, dusting and polishing late into the night. Maybe that was part of it. But maybe, too, the touches we think of as homey for dementia—Oasis was packed with these: rugs, doilies, pictures, curios, side and end tables, puffy chairs—are, sooner or later, not just physically awkward and potentially dangerous (bumps, scrapes, falls) but mentally taxing as well. So much to take in, so much to process and comprehend. Sensory off-loading becomes a mercy. Low light and stillness work best when Mary becomes distressed. A quiet voice, a hand on her forehead.

~

Almost always, now, she will accept such simple touch. Not just accept but tuck into gladly, rooting to the warmth. It is the same with most of the residents on her floor, completing a process begun years ago. A process of departure, and return.

There are these terrible gifts. They come with ending. Terrible, seven years ago, to see Bill, my father, turned into a sleeping statue, never to awaken. But a gift finally to just touch again his cheek, forehead, hair, as once I must have done.

Touch is the rock. You return to it. You're permitted to return to it.

It's no small thing.

~

The great happiness of caregiving, its frequent gift, is to be where you're supposed to be. (Instinct tells me to say this to you now. Instinct structures all these late messages.)

Not where things are easy, or satisfactorily achieved, or achievable, or even necessarily pleasant.

But where you ought to be, have to be, and are. It brings a peace.

A peace that can interrogate, with soft insistence, all the un-peace elsewhere in your life: *Where is it you're supposed to be?*

~

Angling cups to lips, slipping spoonfuls past teeth, lowering bedrails, fastening Velcro straps—so many moments when you wonder, *How long can you call an institution home?*

And hear the answer clear, from deep within your bones: *A long, long time. A lifetime, even.*

You know then, again, how much you will miss this when it's gone. Not just her or him. *This*. When will your heart be so on-duty again?

(And what will occupy a demobilized heart?)

~

If I have less to say about Mary's time at Stillwater, it is not because it has been less eventful. Momentous change sweeps her along, more swiftly, or at least more visibly, than ever.

She has weathered physical illnesses that seemed bound to carry her away—a whole summer vomiting white froth, shrinking to a skeleton—and come back. Gasping sessions, clutching her chest.

Staff marvel at her physical strength and stamina. Strong teeth, all her own. Incredibly acute hearing. Vision that is actually improving, no one knows how. A will that still sees her shuffling, once a day, a few steps with her walker in her room. All this, what she used to call her "farmgirl stock", ensuring that she will see all of dementia, with no early exit.

Having bored down through memory, language, thinking and feeling, dementia is now at work in the basement, taking apart the machinery that permits motor movement, correct perception, and reflexes like swallowing and awareness of pain. She struggles on every front, usually with calm doggedness, often with a smile.

She sees things that aren't there, or at least that we don't see. "Girls" in the room, "a lady" or "a man" standing or moving among us. She becomes insistent, sometimes upset, when others don't see them. Sometimes she can't see anything, it seems. Her eyes glaze over and she looks blind. Perhaps she is. She stares approximately at things, unfocused, unseeing.

She screams occasionally, kicks or slaps. Cries suddenly, sometimes at length.

And yet a gained and gaining peace appears to hold, uniting these myriad outbreaks and alarms.

~

You have to try, as a caregiver, not to impose your story on the stories. You want your story of good care to strengthen, to prevail. You may be tempted to shout it to believe in it.

At Stillwater, what looks like finally getting it right is actually, or also, the peace of subsidence. It takes energy to fight or keep fighting. It takes energy to get or stay angry. It takes energy to be or stay acutely unhappy. That energy is dwindling.

~

And yet. And even so. Mary calls the view of the Walmart parking lot *beautiful*. She says this person is *good*. That person is *so nice*. She says the padded vinyl table of her wheelchair, the one she cleans and polishes all day with a pressing, circling hand—is *a lovely table*.

She has said these kinds of things all through. *A lucky girl*. She says them more now.

Hearing them, you can wonder: Am I hearing a vulnerable and almost powerless person tell herself her world is, after all, benign?

Am I hearing the drastic simplifications of dementia?

Or am I hearing, perhaps, the simple truth? What has been carried back from the other side, the depths. A scattering of feelings and values, held together by a story that is her own achievement, and wholly remarkable. *I love housekeeping*: this wheelchair and its table are my house.

Don't worry so much about meaning, I read once in a book on dream interpretation. Meaning is shy. *Listen to how the person talks about it. Look at how they look.*

Mary speaks calmly, cheerfully at these times. Her gaze is calm and steady.

~

She has family again. Lots of them. A *tall guy*. A *girl*. A lot of *she*s: Klara, who saves her an extra piece of cake at night. Lucille, who hugs and fusses over her, calling her Mama.

Her most important family member is Dalisay. An agency PSW who met Mary at Oasis, Dalisay is with her from one to nine p.m., six days a week. They have formed a remarkable bond, tested often, sometimes severely, but strong with love and knowledge. Dalisay is *my girl*.

Her new family is paid to be with her. Paid, but also freely giving. They give her pats, hugs, kisses, laughter, time. Dalisay buys her a pair of slippers on her day off, a jar of the peanuts Mary likes on her way in.

What family is not free and paid for?

Mary grew up in a farm family of nine. Then lived in a dorm filled with nursing students, with a roommate, for five years. She married and started a family that grew to seven. A busy, bustling house for twenty, twenty-five years. Then came quieter, darker times. An emptying house. Depression. Drinking. *I need people*. She has always needed, and mostly lived in, a big family. Now she does again.

~

Dalisay is not a perfect employee. (Do yourself a favour, early on, and stop looking for these.) She shows up late, no matter how many times I remind her. We disagree on some other issues. But she has ways with Mary that are lovely and that catch at my heart no matter how many times I see them.

The natural way she touches Mary's arm, the way old friends touch, when they are sitting together by the front window, watching the squirrels, or by the window in the library, watching the cars and trucks in the parking lot of Agincourt Mall.

When I arrive at Mary's room and hear them together in the bathroom—"Stand up now, dear"; "Turn, no, this way, dear"— I get a lump in my throat and feel immensely reassured. *The buck stops here*, I said once to Sue. It is a good credo for any caregiving. Find whatever family you need, get them however you can, and give the man, the woman, the care they finally deserve.

What I especially treasure in Dalisay is her respect for Mary's intelligence. That has been a surprise and a perpetual delight. "She's so smart," Dalisay says, and means it.

She understands the enormous ingenuity it takes to solve dementia's riddles, to sit its wicked long exam. It asks for genius to get through a quarter-hour. To eat a snack when your distance perception is telling you the plate is somewhere it isn't, your fingers are moving unreliably, and your mouth is fighting through a storm of noise to catch the correct signals for the sequence of open, draw in, close, chew, swallow.

She understands, especially, that Mary's non-stop stream of words and syllables and growls and hums and trills, interspersed with faces and gestures, are talk, language, story, Mary's lifelong treasure.

She knows that "you", now, sometimes means you and sometimes means I. "You are," she will say, meaning *I am.* "Did you?" Meaning, *I did?* It doesn't sound peculiar, but somehow, strangely, right. If I am not I, perhaps you are I. And you, usually, are "she".

~

The other day, the three of us were visiting in Mary's room. Mary in her wheelchair, Dalisay and I sitting on either side. After telling a long story with sounds, laughter and gesticulations—I caught a little of the gist of it—Mary's speech began to slow. She pointed vaguely at the bed, saying what sounded like "fix it" or "fix thing". The gesture perhaps indicated the floor in front of the bed. Dalisay and I peered to find a crumb or scrap of paper, which Mary often spots and wants us to pick up. Then she said "she", pointing at the air beside the bed, and I thought she was seeing one of her "ladies" or "girls", appearances that sometimes herald agitation and distress.

But, no. Dalisay got it before I did. She wanted, Dalisay explained, to go to bed for a nap. We transferred her and, sure enough, she dropped off right away. Out in the hall, I asked Dalisay how she'd known. "She means herself … standing on the floor," she said.

The "she" she'd been indicating, above the floor, beside the bed, was herself, some moments hence, standing where she would be on her way to bed.

Really? Dalisay nodded vigorously.

I left feeling peaceful, as if carried on a warm wave. It was one of the times I was sure that Mary was wrapped in a net of care, a net that held me too. There is such a purity sometimes to the consolations of caregiving—when, after so much worry for so long, the worry stops, and you know that all that can and should be done has been done and done well. It feels like the pleasant heaviness that comes after a long day of physical work.

Sparrows were chittering in the ivy on the wall by the parking lot. A cold day, the morning frost still glittering in mid-afternoon.

~

If any of this makes Mary seem a special case, some kind of Alzheimer's savant, then I've failed (or you have). Time and again, I've seen the other residents achieve something similar: persistence of meaning by their own means. Often new, often startling means. You have to know the person, know their language. If I knew them better, I would see it far more.

~

On another frosty day, when it snapped cold a couple of weeks ago, I arrived at Stillwater a little late. Driving over, I was thinking that Mary had lived there almost twenty months. Around a year and a half, all along, had been her time to move to a new place. Would she pass soon? Was there another home than death beyond this? Her mother died from a heart attack at eighty-eight, walking home from church in Moose Jaw. Mary is ninety-one, and has taken a heart pill since her early seventies.

Dalisay and Mary were sitting by the front window, watching the squirrels as they waited for me. "You see," Dalisay said to her, "the tall guy is back. The tall guy always comes."

Dalisay grew up in the Philippines, and her lilting pronunciations please and exasperate Mary, though she has learned them too.

Mary glanced at me and returned to watching Dalisay. She is her anchor these days, her main *she*.

We fell into comfortable banter, comparing our days. Mary jabbed her finger at the glass: there, there, there. "She wants me to pick up the leaves," Dalisay said. We smiled. Mary's housekeeping fetish is an old motif, a shared joke, sometimes the start of an argument as Mary badgers Dalisay to pick up tiny specks from the floor. The many fallen leaves have made an unsightly green floor, sometimes so intolerable that they have to go and find a different view.

Now a squirrel came hopping by. Mary pointed at it excitedly. "That thing!" She watched it closely. "Do you want us to pick him up too?" I said. Mary glared, affronted. "It's his!"

Belatedly, I was catching up to a unity forming, a unified scene that made me reel a little. "Things" (leaves) were building up, needing to be picked up, on the green floor (grass) of her home, which she shared with another thing (squirrel). And now, as if to complete the picture, she warbled a little tune, a handful of notes up and down. "She hears that thing," Dalisay said. Another thing —"What thing?" I asked. "That sound." And then, cocking my head, I caught it faintly. An alto whine from a machine, a vacuum cleaner perhaps, in a room down the hall. Mary's little descant had accompanied it.

She has it all here, I realized. Nature, Language, Company, Music. Her family story. You can't find more, or less, than you are, wherever you are. She was here, and so her story was here, despite everything. Altered, chopped, rearranged.

Still whole. Still her own.

~

Yesterday she insisted on drinking her juice herself, immediately spilling it over her clothes and chair. She became distraught and remained so for the next half-hour, until I got her into bed and she fell into an exhausted sleep. "I can't ... do before," she said several times. "Not ... what I was."

Her words so clear.
Unmissable.

~

Another afternoon, when I am asking a doctor about her purple-white fingertips and constant pressings on the tabletop, she says plainly, "Numb."

As a decade of dementia rolls away like a boulder.

~

One day, it took a team of us to dry her tears. When I arrived, she was sitting in her chair to one side of the bowling circle, crying inconsolably. Dalisay could not settle her, nor could I. Laura brought her back into the circle to try again. She tried to guide, with words and gestures: push the ball down the slide, hit the white pins with the girl beside them. But she also teased and joshed: Oh, boo hoo hoo, there you go again. Mary couldn't see through her tears and fright. She looked wildly about, swinging her head back and forth amid the blurs of colours, shapes and noise.

Lucille came in and wrapped her arms around her. Kissed her on the cheek, murmuring endearments. But even from her Mary pulled away, panic in her face.

By accident, when she thrust her hands out as if to push the world away, she sent the ball down the metal rails and across the floor into the pins, spilling them. But the cheers and claps this brought alarmed her even more, redoubling her tears.

Quiet time in the TV room was the only help. Somebody brought juice and a mini-muffin. I sat beside her, holding her hand, patting her back. Soon she was laughing at cartoons on TVO Kids. Pointing at the characters, talking about them in a rush of sounds I couldn't understand.

Dalisay came back from changing the bed and said that she would take Mary downstairs to watch the squirrels.

Driving to work afterwards, I heard, in a radio interview, the word *goodment*. It was said by a personal trainer, who was describing her approach to exercise. Forget the gym, forget weights and machines, forget measuring your improvement. Accept your body as it is and move enjoyably.

"Do it for the goodment of yourself," she said.

Goodment? Had I heard her correctly? Did she mean betterment?

But, no. A minute later, she said, "others' goodment". No mistake.

The interview ended, I switched off the radio. But the word—*goodment*—remained, switched on and just beginning. Establishing itself, the way a new word will, so that soon it seems like an old word lost and regained. With uses you can't see how you ever did without.

Goodment. Good meant, i.e., intended. *—ment*, denoting a state or condition, as in betterment (but not comparative, i.e., not better than anything, already good). *—ment*, denoting mind, e.g., mental, contrast with dement, dementia.

For the goodment of others.

    For the goodment of yourself.

           ~

It's late now, later than I intended. I'll close with a few words that I wrote to myself on another late night, not long ago, after a long and painfully mistaken day. The kind of day that reminds you that caregiving produces seniors but no graduates.

I keep the words on a folded slip of paper in my wallet, though in writing them down already I had them by heart.

           ~

Be something harder to be than everyone, no one, or anyone.

    Be someone.

    Not everywhere, elsewhere, nowhere.

    Here.

Not always, never, or eventually.
Now.

~

Be something harder to be than a father or mother,
brother or sister, husband or wife, son or daughter.
Be a friend.

~

For the goodment of others.
For the goodment of yourself.

Be with.

for Mary

Also by Mike Barnes

Short Story Collections
Aquarium (1999)
Contrary Angel (2004)
The Reasonable Ogre:
Tales for the Sick and Well (2012)

Novels
The Syllabus (2002)
Catalogue Raisonné (2005)
The Adjustment League (2016)

Non-Fiction
The Lily Pond (2008)

Poetry Collections
Calm Jazz Sea (1996)
A Thaw Foretold (2006)